HOWZAT!

Hadlee's tales from the boundary

Sir Richard Hadlee

REED

Established in 1907, Reed Publishing (NZ) Ltd
is New Zealand's largest book publisher, with over 300 titles in print.

For details on all these books visit our website:
www.reed.co.nz

Published by Reed Books, a division of Reed Publishing (NZ) Ltd,
39 Rawene Rd, Birkenhead, Auckland.
Associated companies, branches and representatives throughout the world.

ISBN 0 7900 0880 7

Designed by Graeme Leather
Cover designed by Serena Kearns
Cover photograph by Ross Setford

First published 2002

Printed in New Zealand

Contents

the characters

growing up with the game

touring

the commentators and the media

extras

Biography

Richard Hadlee, born in Christchurch in 1951, played cricket for Canterbury 1971–90, Tasmania 1979–80, Nottinghamshire 1978–87 and New Zealand 1972–90. In 1981 he was awarded an MBE for services to New Zealand sport and in 1990 a knighthood for services to cricket. He was named New Zealand Sportsman of the Year in 1980 and 1986, New Zealand Sportsperson of the Last 25 Years in 1987 and New Zealand Sportsperson of the Decade in 1989.

He played 86 test matches and 115 one-day internationals and captured 431 test wickets (a world record until it was surpassed by Kapil Dev). His best bowling performance was 9/52 against Australia at the Gabba in 1985–86. He scored 3124 test runs at an average of 27.16; his highest test score was 151 not out against Sri Lanka.

On 4 February 1990, on his home ground of Lancaster Park in Christchurch, Richard Hadlee became the first bowler in test history to capture 400 test wickets. The great Sir Don Bradman once described him as 'the master of rhythm and swing'.

Sir Richard is now an ambassador for the Bank of New Zealand, a professional speaker, a Level III cricket coach and chairman of selectors of the New Zealand cricket team. He also imports and distributes Hadlee memorabilia and cricket equipment.

history
and
histrionics

Not out!

Dr W.G. Grace, the grandfather of world cricket, was a law unto himself. He broke the majority of rules and stunned his team-mates and the opposition innumerable times. On one occasion when he was batting he reached 93 then declared the innings closed. He later explained to his team that 93 was the only score between 0 and 100 that he had not yet made.

On another occasion he lofted the ball into the air and, before the catch had been taken, declared the innings closed. The umpire was forced to give him 'not out' on the grounds that the ball had been caught after the declaration.

A civil war

Cricket in Victoria, Canada, hasn't always been regarded as the genteel sport it is today. While some people have viewed cricketers as tea-slurping men in white, in 1858 the pitch at Beacon Hill bore witness to a fatal incident after two players had a serious misunderstanding. John Collins and William Morris settled their dispute from ten paces, with pistols. Three shots were exchanged before Collins was 'bowled' for his final innings and sent to the great wicket-keeper in the sky. Morris fled the country.

News of the bloody exchange shocked the citizens of Victoria, who at least knew where to fix the blame for such lawlessness — both men were Americans.

Time for a prayer

The Reverend David Shepherd played for England as an opening batsman during the 1960s, and later became Archbishop of Canterbury. His batting record was good, with three test centuries in his 1172 test runs, and an average of 37.8. Shepherd also stood at first slip to the fast bowlers, and while he caught many catches, he also dropped a few.

Fred Trueman, the great Yorkshire and England fast bowler who played in the 1950s and 1960s, was always ready to comment on the abilities of the minister, on one occasion saying, 'You might have kept your eyes closed when you were praying, Vicar, but I wish you would keep them open when you batted and when I bowled.'

A driving sort of innings

The actor Trevor Howard, who appeared on screen in many war movies, was an ardent cricket follower but a player of only moderate ability. Howard was so keen on the game that one day in 1960 he got up at 5 a.m. and drove almost 300 km from London to play in a match at Buxton, in Derbyshire, only to be out first ball. After the match he drove back to London.

He will not be the last cricketer to suffer that fate, such is the nature of the game.

Fired out!

Alan Dawson was batting in a match at Kalgoorlie, Australia, in 1970 when he was struck by a delivery that ignited a box of matches in his pocket. As he was jumping about in and around the batting crease in an attempt to put out the flames, the opposition ran him out.

Who's the best?

Since my retirement from international cricket in 1990 I have retained my involvement with the game in a number of ways, including coaching, playing Presidents grade for High School Old Boys and playing in charity matches, and latterly as a selector. I have also enjoyed being in the radio or television commentary box talking about cricket. My love for the game will continue for the rest of my life.

I am often asked to address schools and do some coaching, and I like to give the youngsters some thoughts on my upbringing in the game, and pass on cricket tips and advice. This is normally followed by a question and answer session. During one such session a youngster asked, 'Who was the best cricketer of all time — Sir Donald Bradman or Dr W.G. Grace?'

I had no hesitation in saying that Bradman was the best batsman of all time, because he had a test batting average of 99.94. However, W.G. Grace was the best all-round cricketer because he scored nearly 55,000 runs, including 126 centuries, and captured nearly 3000 wickets in first-class cricket.

Another young fellow said, as quick as a flash, 'I guess you would know, sir. You played against them both.'

Another time, I was recalling my upbringing and said that I had lived and breathed cricket night and day. I was so keen that I could recall the names of all the players who had played test cricket for New Zealand. One of the youngsters piped up, 'It was easy for you to remember the players' names, sir, because there were only 30 players who had played test cricket for New Zealand way back then.'

Someone else added, 'Yeah, that's right. It's harder for us to remember all those who have played for New Zealand because now there are over 200 players to remember. In your day you played with them all, so it was easy to recall all the names.'

A scorer's dilemma

Each year a charity cricket match is played at St Kevin's College, Melbourne, to raise money for the Multiple Sclerosis Society of Victoria. An Old World XI plays an Old Australian XI, with players of the 1970s and the 1980s coming together to play a 30-over match. During the 1990s I played in seven of these matches, and in 1998 $200,000 was raised.

The captain of the World XI team that year was Barry Richards, the great South African batsman. Richards put a copy of the batting order up in the dressing room so the players could prepare themselves mentally for the task in the middle, and another copy was sent to Mary, the fastidious scorer. I sometimes wonder what she thought when the piece of paper arrived and she went to enter the names in the scorebook. The players were listed as follows:

1. 'Dav' [Dav Whatmore (Sri Lanka/Australia)]
2. 'Arkle' [Derek Randall (England), named for the racehorse Arkle]

3. 'Guru' [Asanka Gurusinha (Sri Lanka)]

4. 'Captain' [Barry Richards (South Africa)]

5. 'Gus' [Augustine Logi (West Indies)]

6. 'Kingdom' [Collis King (West Indies)]

7. 'Paddles' [Sir Richard Hadlee (New Zealand)]

8. 'Sam' [Athula Samarasekera (Sri Lanka)]

9. 'Lancer' [Lance Cairns (New Zealand)]

10. 'Spinner' [Ian Salisbury (England)]

11. 'Bomber' [Colin Croft (West Indies), named 'Bomber' after knocking over umpire Fred Goodall]

12. The Twelfth Man [a local person who bids for the role on the day]

Playing for a cause

The MS charity match is always a lot of fun, and the players do what they can to provide an enjoyable spectacle for the 2000 onlookers who attend. Behind the scenes, well away from the spectators and the sponsors, other things go on that keep the players amused. Many of these cricketers are now in their fifties, some are in their forties, and the odd player may even have reached his sixties.

To prepare the players for the match, the organisers supply physiotherapists and masseurs. Derek Randall decided the massage he received from a female masseuse was so good he went back for three more. Colin Croft had three women attending to his sore muscles, and I had two women attending a calf muscle strain I had picked up in a practice match. Barry Richards arrived in Melbourne limping after being hit on the shin by a ball from his son, and needed treatment to help get him on the field of play. There were more physios and massage therapists than players at the ground. Even in our playing days and in our wildest dreams we had never had that sort of attention or care before. One can only imagine how good we could have been if we had had all that pre-match attention when we were playing seriously.

Jeff Thomson brought his 15-year-old son Matthew to the match, and when he introduced him Thommo said to me, 'Look at his feet.' I couldn't believe my eyes because he took size 17 shoes. When I was at school I was nicknamed 'Paddles' because of my rather large feet, but 'Boats' would have described Matthew's feet.

Lance Cairns and I had arrived in Melbourne on the same flight. As I retrieved my cricket coffin from the conveyer belt I saw Lance standing there with a grip bag over his shoulder. 'Where's your gear?' I asked him.

'There it is,' he said, pointing to a set of golf clubs.

'Is that all you've brought with you?'

'That's all I need to play with,' Lance responded.

'Whose gear are you going to use for the game?'

'Yours,' he said.

Next morning, all the players assembled in the foyer of the Grand Hotel at 11.30 to be driven to the ground. Lance stood there in jandals, shorts and a T-shirt. He was carrying one of the hotel's plastic laundry bags, which contained a pair of cricket socks, a white cricket shirt, a pair of trousers and rubber-soled shoes. He was ready for action! Mind you, strange as he looked, he wasn't alone — six other players were carrying their gear in plastic laundry bags.

For the record, Lance scored one run with the bat, didn't bowl, but shot a 76 off the stick on the golf course.

Most players brought with them heaps of bats that everyone signed. It was a full-time job signing all the mini and full-sized bats that would later be used for charity auctions and other fundraising activities. The people who attend the MS match are mainly sponsors and their guests, who are there to have a good time. Some are knowledgeable, some are less so. After ten overs someone standing in a marquee with a glass of wine in one hand and a beer in the other asked me, 'Who's winning this match?'

The night before the match an official function is held at which the guests bid for the right to be twelfth man and take part in the game. When I was batting towards the end of our innings I hit the Australians' twelfth man for six, with the ball going up onto the freeway and, no doubt, into the city centre on the back of a truck. As a replacement ball was brought onto the field I heard Lennie Pascoe say to the bowler, 'Bounce him, mate!', a typical competitive Aussie comment designed to intimidate the batsman.

I thought, 'No one bowls bouncers in this type of cricket,' with the result that the twelfth man, who bowled at a brisk medium pace, took me unawares. It was a bouncer and I missed it, the ball hitting me rather painfully in the chest. I wasn't going to let the bowler know he had hurt me, however, so I desperately avoided rubbing the affected area, gritted my teeth and faced the final ball of the innings. I quickly dispatched the ball to the boundary for four, and as I walked off the field with the twelfth man I said to him with a smile, 'You have some potential as a fast bowler, but it is important to pitch the ball up and give it a chance to swing in the air and deceive the batsman.'

For the record, Australia won the match off the last ball — their first win in four years.

Time for a change!

Over the years a number of New Zealand sportspeople have been made knights or dames, including Sir Murray Halberg (athletics), Sir Wilson Whineray (rugby), Sir Brian Lochore (rugby), Sir Edmund Hillary (moutaineering), Sir Bob Charles (golf) and Dame Susan Devoy (squash). When changes to the New Zealand Honours List were being considered, a member of the public wrote to the editor of his local newspaper suggesting it would be a good idea to do away with all these honours and formalities. Everyone should be called 'Bro' or 'Sheila', he said.

So we'd have Bro Murray, Bro Wilson, Bro Brian, Bro Ed, Bro Bob and Sheila Sue!

A quick pair

The quickest pair in the history of the game happened in consecutive balls, when Glamorgan's number 11 batsman, Peter Judge, was bowled by India's Sarwate first ball for a duck. The innings was closed and, to save time, as Glamorgan followed on, Judge opened the second innings. He was immediately bowled by Sarwate again.

A Bird's tale

England's Harold 'Dickie' Bird will go down in cricket history as one of the great characters of the game, and one of the best umpires of all time. He was born in Barnsley, Yorkshire, and played first-class cricket for Yorkshire before moving to Leicestershire. While playing for Yorkshire he scored a double century and was then relegated to the second team when Geoff Boycott, who had been on England duty, returned to the team. He later became a universally respected umpire of great quality and integrity.

Dickie had a wonderful rapport with players, but he was also very nervous and had a number of idiosyncrasies and mannerisms, which often led to amusing incidents. In 1970, when he was playing for Yorkshire against Surrey at The Oval, London, he arrived at the ground at 5.30 a.m., nearly six hours before the start of play. Since the gates were locked he climbed them, to be accosted by a surprised policeman.

On another occasion Dickie was invited by Her Majesty the Queen to attend a luncheon at Buckingham Palace. He arrived at the palace in time for breakfast, only to be advised that he was too early for lunch. He then whiled away the next five hours in a nearby café drinking many cups of tea until it was time to go back to the palace.

During his playing days Dickie was so nervous that he once buckled his pads to each other and fell flat on his face as he walked out to bat. There were other times when he went missing, only to be found by his team-mates locked away in the toilet. A wonderful man and a great character — the game needs more people like Dickie Bird.

Hero for zero

Godfrey Evans, an England wicket-keeper, held a unique record of batting 97 minutes in a test match before scoring his first run. He achieved that feat against Australia at the Adelaide Oval in 1946/47 and eventually went on to score ten.

The record stood for 53 years before New Zealand's Geoff Allott made his way into the history books by smashing the world record by four minutes, before being dismissed without scoring against South Africa at Eden Park in March 1999.

Allott's innings was a very valuable one, however, because South Africa amassed 621/5 and New Zealand were in trouble and struggling at 320/9, still 102 runs short of the follow-on mark. When Allott was eventually dismissed New Zealand were out for 352, but by batting as long as he did he made it easier for New Zealand to bat out the last day to save the match. It was a vital last-wicket partnership with Chris Harris, who ended up 68 not out.

In the commentary box there was a lot of banter as Allott moved towards the record. I had also sponsored Geoff and he had 'Hadlee Cricket' stickers plastered all over his bat. He was using a 'Master Class' bat that attracted some comment as he deliberately pushed another ball back to the bowler. Ian Smith said, 'That bat must be made of balsa wood because Geoff Allott can't hit the ball off the square.'

Allott kept playing dead bat shots ball after ball, and he never looked like scoring a run. His job was to survive and support Harry.

In the commentary box with Smithy was former New Zealand opening batsman and captain John Wright. At one stage Peter Marriott, the television statistician, handed Smithy a piece of paper and said, 'Geoff Allott is now approaching the New Zealand record for time spent at the crease before scoring a run. That record is currently held by John Wright, who batted 66 minutes against Australia at the Basin Reserve in Wellington in 1981/82. Wright went on to score 38 — and it took him three weeks to score those runs.'

Wrighty had the final word before going to a commercial break, quipping, 'And everyone went to sleep.' While the commercials were playing, however, Wrighty said off air, 'Is that record really mine?' (In fact,

Martin Snedden had the dubious honour of batting 94 minutes without scoring a run against Australia in 1989/90.)

As Geoff Allott went on to break Wrighty's record, the ground announcer advised the crowd of his feat and Allott raised his bat, the South African fielders applauded and Harry congratulated him on his record. Thirty-four minutes later this was repeated as Allott, having faced and survived 77 balls, broke Evans' record. At the after-match press conference Allott commented, 'It was the only chance that I would ever get to salute the crowd, so I thought, what the hell.'

It was great television exposure for the Hadlee bat until Smithy asked for the cameras to pan in on the bat again, saying, 'Allott must have won that bat in a raffle, because it doesn't score any runs.' Fortunately Wrighty came to my rescue, responding, 'It must have been an expensive raffle. That bat will be worth millions now that it is part of a world record.'

A case of foot and mouth

Robert Muldoon, New Zealand's prime minister at the time of the 'underarm incident' at the MCG on 1 February 1981, was not impressed with Australia's tactics. With New Zealand needing six runs to tie the match, the Australian captain, Greg Chappell, instructed his younger brother, Trevor, to bowl the last ball of the match underarm to Brian McKechnie. A political war developed between the two countries. Muldoon saw the incident as an act of cowardice, commenting, 'It was appropriate the Australians were dressed in yellow.'

Greg Chappell's popularity was tarnished all over the world through his action, but he probably gained some sympathy from his diehard supporters after Muldoon's comments. Several days after the incident, a disease was detected on a New Zealand farm. Some Australians thought it was rather appropriate that there was an outbreak of foot and mouth in New Zealand.

A world rating at last!

Chris Cowdrey, the son of Lord Cowdrey, captained Kent and England. He recalls the story of when he played his first one-day international. It was 1985, and England was playing Australia at the MCG.

'Ninety-two thousand people were packed into the ground, with 91,000 supporting Australia, there were 500 from Hong Kong and 500 from Mike Burton's tour party from Gloucester.

'We got off to one of our better starts — we were 85/5. I was walking out to bat, somewhat apprehensive, but I was still expectant of scoring some runs and helping my country out of a difficult situation. As I entered the war zone the crowd roared and I could hear them saying, "Kill, kill, kill; knock his … head off."

'I was greeted by Mike Gatting, who was on 45, and he said to me, "Craig McDermott is angling the ball down the leg side, so get your body across and work the ball down to fine leg for a single to get off the mark and give me the strike."

'"OK," I said.

'So I faced the first ball, shuffled across the stumps as I was told to do, missed it and I was out lbw first ball.

'"Bugger it," I thought. "I've let the team down."

'I walked back to the pavilion and the crowd roared again. As a professional player I was paid to score runs, and I felt I had failed. The thought came quickly that if I looked at the edge of my bat, people would think that I had got a bad decision and that I was unlucky.

'The crowd roared again as the giant television screen showed the replay of the dismissal five times and I could see each time that I was out plumb lbw. I kept walking as quickly as I could, but I could see out of the corner of my eye my career statistics flash onto the screen — "one match, one innings, no runs, highest score zero, average 0.00". There was another roar from the crowd as that f… little duck walked across the screen. Then I saw my world ranking flash onto the screen and I was at number 119. I thought that was quite good under the circumstances, but I soon realised that there were only seven teams in international cricket and Devon Malcolm was rated last at number 120.

'As I walked up the steps someone yelled out, "Hey Cowdrey, your father was a fat git as well."

'It was certainly not an innings to remember.'

Tickets please

At times players and commentators have had difficulty getting into grounds because the security staff, who know nothing about the game, have rigidly enforced the rule 'No ticket, no entry to the ground.'

On one occasion a minibus in which I was travelling with Jeremy Coney, Martin Crowe and John Wright was detained at the gate while the driver argued with the guard, until finally common sense prevailed.

A few years later, it was 9 a.m. at Eden Park and the commentators were arriving at the ground to do the pre-match interviews and assess the playing conditions. There was only a handful of spectators at the ground, along with a few officials and the television crew doing their jobs. There were also a few security guards, who were dressed resplendently in the Eden Park blue, red and white tracksuits. One guard was positioned inside the rope surrounding the main playing area to protect the test pitch. Martin Crowe, who was by then a television and radio commentator, strolled onto the playing arena and headed for the pitch area to get some thoughts as to who should bat or bowl first if they won the toss. As he stepped over the rope to inspect the pitch he was asked by the guard, 'Do you have a pass, sir?'

'I am part of the commentary team,' Martin replied.

'I am sorry, sir, I have my instructions. You do not have a pass, so please step back over the rope.'

Ian Smith then arrived. Smithy has two dominant traits — he has a strong sense of humour and he doesn't take fools lightly. The guard asked whether Smithy had a pass. Ian, being Ian, said 'No.' There now began a series of questions and answers, with no one prepared to budge an inch.

Smithy finally turned to the guard and said, 'If I can't come in here to inspect the pitch, you will have to come with me up to the television box, get behind a microphone and tell thousands of people in New Zealand and in other parts of the world what the pitch is going to do for the next five days, because you are the only person who has seen it.'

The guard was still not prepared to move, simply saying, 'Please step back behind the rope, sir.'

By this time Smithy was extremely frustrated. Noticing the groundsman's dog sitting at one end of the pitch he said sarcastically, 'Has the dog got a pass?'

'Please step behind the rope, sir.'

'Look,' said Smithy. 'There are going to be two guys out here wearing helmets soon and I'll bet you they don't have passes, so will you stop them? There will also be two blokes with white coats and hats, so will they be stopped as well? Then there will be a big guy wanting to run in with a ball in his hand, so will you stop him as well? You will be the only person out here, which won't be a lot of fun for the millions of people watching you doing nothing! But at least you will be very famous!'

'Sir, I have told you before, please step back behind the rope,' said the conscientious guard.

Smithy finally stormed off in search of an official, who later advised the security guard that he would be better employed taking care of the thousands of drunken spectators, of whom there were none at 9.30 a.m.

Just another mix-up

'Bomber' Wells was a well-known English county cricketer in the 1950s. He was a good spin bowler who took a lot of wickets with one of the shortest run-ups in the game. He took one pace and it was said that he bowled an over in a village match while the clock struck twelve.

As a batsman he had a few deficiencies, especially when running between the wickets. He and Sam Cook, his other spin bowler, were described as being 'very eccentric' when they batted together. Things were so bad that the club fined them a half-crown every time one of them was run out. During yet another mix-up Sam yelled out to Bomber, 'For God's sake call!'

To which Bomber replied, 'Heads!'

Letters to the champions

On 12 November 1988 I became the leading wicket-taker in the history of test cricket, surpassing Ian Botham's record. Arun Lal became my 374th victim when he was caught by Chris Kuggeleijn at slip for six at Bangalore, India.

Six years later Kapil Dev equalled my world record of 431 test wickets at Bangalore, and later broke it at Ahmedabad, India, when Hashan Tillercaratne was caught by the wicket-keeper down the leg side. When Kapil equalled my record I sent him this message:

Dear Kapil

Congratulations on equalling my world record — a fantastic effort and well deserved.

In previous communications, I've mentioned your stamina, fitness, skill and now you have been totally rewarded for your efforts.

Your next wicket (next ball!) will be a very special moment in your career and in world cricket. Records are meant to be broken and perhaps someone else will go beyond your achievements, but to be a pace setter is something I enjoyed immensely.

You now become number one — cherish the moment and be thankful for what the game has offered and given you.

All the best, my friend.

Regards

Richard

Kapil went on to capture 434 test wickets before retiring.

When West Indian fast bowler Courtney Walsh joined us with 400 or more test wickets in March 1999, I faxed this message to him in Trinidad:

Dear Courtney

Congratulations on reaching 400 test wickets. You have now joined an 'exclusive' club restricted to three people. May you go on and achieve more wickets and perhaps become our 'President'.

In due course, you will receive your first account for subscriptions, so that we can meet and discuss further bowlers who should be admitted to the club!!

Regards

Richard Hadlee, 'Treasurer'!!

The Gentlemen of Yorkshire

The Yorkshire Gentlemen are a team who take great pride in the tradition of the game. The players arrive at 11 a.m. in their Rolls-Royces, BMWs or Mercedes for an 11.30 start. Lunch is taken from 1.30 to 2.10. All the players look resplendent in their club blazers and ties. Clean whites and the club sweater and cap are worn on the field of play, and the players do the mandatory warm-ups and have some throw-downs before the start of play. The 'Gentlemen' don't toss to decide who should bat or bowl first, because they don't have a coin — they carry only notes. When the opposition arrive, they are informed that they are in the field first.

On this particular day one of the players, who goes by the name of Johnathan Dudley-Smith Parsons, arrived in his chaffeur-driven

Rolls-Royce with his labrador puppy, Hancock. The dog obediently responded to any commands it received: 'Hancock, fetch the stick,' 'Hancock, fetch the ball,' 'Come here, Hancock, sit, stay, down boy, good boy.' Dudley-Smith Parsons, who was not renowned for his batting ability, or his bowling for that matter, went out to bat and was bowled first ball. As he returned to the pavilion one of his team-mates remarked, 'Thou should have sent Hancock out to bat.'

Sorry ladies!

While I was in England for the 1999 World Cup I played in a charity six-a-side cricket match in Bath. To my delight, the organisers asked me to play as a special guest for the Somerset Ladies Wanderers cricket team, and I looked forward to what would certainly be an interesting and different experience.

During the day we won two matches against men's teams, which really pleased the women. In fact, we had some useful players, especially Rachel Lloyd, who won the all-rounder of the day award and the prize for the best fielding moment of the day when she ran a batsman out from 40 m with a direct hit. Several other young women impressed with the bat and the ball during the day. Although it wasn't really a surprise to me that we had some success, some of the men's teams may have felt a little embarrassed.

Our first match was against the lads from the successful Bath Rugby Club. They had some very fit and athletic young men, who were keen to impress. They batted first and scored 52, which looked like being too much for the Somerset Ladies to match. We started well, however, and I was asked to face the last over of the match needing 18 to win, a big assignment. I managed to hit a four, then a six, ran two, got a leg-bye, my partner scrambled a bye, and we needed four to win off the last ball. The ball was duly dispatched back past the bowler for the required four, much to the delight of the cheering crowd and the ladies' team. It was a remarkable win.

As we left the field the Bath rugby players were very gracious in defeat, congratulating us on our victory. Then I overheard one of the rugby players comment to a friend on the boundary, 'It wasn't fair. One of the players in the ladies' team had a moustache — and they had Richard Hadlee playing for them as well.'

The 'spittle' position

Peter Walker, a former Glamorgan and England player, was a big man, standing at six foot four inches (193 cm). An orthodox left-arm spin bowler and middle-order batsman, he captured 834 first-class wickets at 28.63, scored nearly 18,000 runs at 26, and held on to 697 catches. He also played three tests for England, averaging 32 with the bat and taking five catches, but he failed to capture a test wicket.

Peter always said he was very grateful that his father lived for the game of cricket, commenting, 'I wouldn't be here today if it wasn't for a rain-delayed match.'

Relating the story of the first match he played for Glamorgan as a 19-year-old, Peter recalled how after each over his captain, Wilfred Wooller, kept sending him from third man at one end of the ground to fine leg at the other end. This eventually began to get to Peter, as he started to tire. On one occasion he left the third man position before the end of the over to ensure he would be in the fine leg position at the start of the next. After the completion of another over he passed his captain, who was standing near the batsman's wickets, and asked, 'Where would you like me to field now, skipper?'

'Young man, I don't care where you field,' Wooller replied. 'Just spit, and where the spit ends up, go and field there.'

Peter, who as a young professional had been taught never to question the captain or a senior player, did as he was told. The spittle ended up in the leg slip area, so he stood in that position and three balls later took a brilliant diving catch. He then spent the rest of his playing days specialising in that area, going on to become one of the finest fielders in that position.

A quick fetch

During the late 1970s the Derbyshire County Cricket Club employed the services of the great South African all-rounder Eddie 'Bunter' Barlow. Bunter was a very tough competitor who demanded total commitment from all the players. In previous years Derby had been the whipping boys of county cricket, and Bunter's task was to create a professional environment at the club, to get the players to lift their performances and to turn them into a more competitive unit.

Bunter felt his players needed to increase their work ethic, which meant they had to be a lot fitter. On each of the non-playing days they had to run long distances, and Bunter would set them targets and guidelines — for example, on one day they had to run $3\frac{1}{2}$ miles (5.6 km) in 17 minutes.

Mike Hendrick, a very accomplished and successful seam bowler who played for England, was asked what he thought of the Bunter

Barlow regime. 'We are a very fit team,' he said. 'If one of the opposition batsmen is able to hit the ball three and a half miles, we'll be able to fetch the ball far quicker than anyone else.'

Village cricket at its best

I am often asked to play in testimonial or benefit cricket matches for players who have given loyal service to their counties in England. During the 1999 World Cup year Basher Hassan, a former Nottinghamshire player who was born in Kenya, asked me play in a match at Milton, north Nottinghamshire. Basher's International XI were playing the local village team to celebrate their fiftieth anniversary and to raise funds for the club.

I said I would be delighted to play, and asked Basher the usual questions — what time do we start, where is the ground, and who is playing? Basher replied that it was a 2.30 start, we would play a 25-over match, and that several of the Notts cricketers I had played with during my time with the team would be playing. These included Clive Rice, Mike Smedley, Pete Hacker, Trevor Tunnicliffe, Bill Taylor and Chris Curzon. I duly put the date in my diary, looking forward to the match on 18 June at the Milton Cricket Club.

A day before the match I went to Trent Bridge to pick up my mail and to get some final directions on how to get to the Milton ground. While I was there I came across an advertisement in a local newspaper stating that the match would be starting at 1.30, that the gates would open at noon, and that it was a 40-over game. I felt a little uneasy about the arrangements at this point, especially since I could not contact Basher, who was at Ascot for the day.

The next morning I arrived at Trent Bridge and met Basher, who reiterated that the game was scheduled to start at 2.30 p.m. and that we would be playing a 25-over match. He then rang the organisers, who said that the match would start at 1.30 as advertised, and that it would be 40 overs. At this stage Basher began to get a little rattled, because he had told all the players to be at the ground for 2.30.

In the meantime, Pete Hacker could not be found, so he was a non-starter, Trevor Tunnicliffe had pulled out of the match owing to work commitments, Bill Taylor had fallen off a ladder and twisted an ankle, and Ricey was in doubt because he had injured a knee at training. We had lost half the team before a ball had been bowled. However, Basher said, Ricey, who was manager of the Notts County team, would send over some of the young professionals on the Notts staff to ensure we had a full complement of players.

The trip from Nottingham to Milton usually takes about 40 minutes, so my wife Di and I set off in plenty of time to get to the ground. We had gone about 15 km when we were passed by a minibus with 'Notts County Cricket Club' on the side. There were three young players dressed in whites in the bus, so we decided to follow it, assuming it would lead us to the ground. The instructions Basher had given us were a little vague — 'Head down the A614 and join the A1; follow the A1 signs north to Retford, but before reaching Retford go off on a slip road; find the signs to Milton, and the cricket club is in a farm, where you wind down a dirt road through the house and the barns.'

We followed the bus for 50 minutes, then as it kept going past Retford I said to Di, 'This isn't right. We've come too far.' Soon after that the bus pulled up at a fish and chip shop, so we stopped and asked the lads whether they were going to Milton.

'No,' they said. 'We're off to a school just out of Retford to coach some youngsters.'

Back in the car we got, and headed back to the main road with a new set of directions. We finally arrived at the cricket ground at 1.15. I was the first of our team to arrive. The opposition were dressed in whites and doing their warm-ups. There were a couple of hundred spectators at the ground, sitting in their deck chairs and enjoying the warmer weather that had just arrived. A marquee had been erected and the scene looked spectacular. The only problem was that we had no players.

I was welcomed by Colin Shaw, the chairman of the Milton Cricket Club, and several other dignitaries, who reminded me that in 1986 the club had organised a benefit match for me. I could not remember the occasion, which was a bit embarrassing, but my photo with the ladies in the tearoom confirmed my presence.

After a while the players in my team started to arrive one by one. First was Mike Smedley, who had been captain of Notts when I played for the club in 1978, and who was now aged 55. The wicket-keeper, Chris Curzon, arrived, followed by two young players from the Notts staff who appeared very keen to play and make an impression. There were now five of us and 13 of them. At this point Colin Shaw said, 'It's 2.20, we need to get this game started. The spectators and the sponsors are restless; perhaps you can toss with the Milton skipper and bat first.'

I agreed that we should bat first, but the toss had to be made in accordance with cricket protocol and the Laws of Cricket. The local photographers gathered round and took pictures of the formalities.

As acting captain I organised the batting order, asking the two young fellows to open the innings, with Curzy to bat at three, Smed at four and me at five. Hopefully the rest of the team would arrive before I went out to bat, otherwise we were in trouble.

The two young fellows looked very smart with all their brand-new sponsored gear. They both decided to wear helmets, which is a little unusual for these types of matches. The opposition were farmers and businessmen from the local village. After the first few overs both batsmen had hardly laid a bat on the ball and they were made to look very ordinary indeed, almost to the point of being embarrassed. Both were eventually dismissed for a few. Curzy played well for his 40, Smed looked good for his 37, and after borrowing some of the opposition's gear I whacked a quickfire 43.

In the meantime, Basher arrived at 2.45, and a limping Bill Taylor carrying a plastic bag with his gear in it had strolled into the ground. Kevin Cooper, a very handy swing bowler for Notts, was a late replacement for Trevor Tunnicliffe, and the balance of the team was made up from the leftovers and non-starters from the Milton Cricket Club team. Ricey, who had withdrawn with an injury, eventually arrived at the ground two hours late after getting lost, but he was in time to cut the birthday cake.

While I was batting, Di was enjoying a conversation with the two young openers. Both youngsters confessed that they were a little embarrassed because they had struggled to hit the ball off the square, while the 'old master' — with the emphasis on 'old' — was hitting sixes into the wheat fields. However, they were encouraging each other with the excuse that they had intended to bat for a short time so the crowd could watch the Internationals. Commenting on my performance, Di added casually, 'He's doing surprisingly well really, because he can't see the ball — his eyes are half shut with a reaction to hayfever.' The gullible youngsters were even more amazed when Di told them that I would be listening to the bowlers' feet as they ran in to bowl, much like a drum beat, and anticipating where the ball would pitch so I could play the appropriate stroke!

The birth of the Bronwydd Cricket Club

On 23 April 1999 I was fortunate to be present at the Bronwydd (pronounced Bronwith) Cricket Club's 21st Anniversary Dinner in Carmarthen, in southwest Wales. Arweyn Thomas, now the club's groundsman, delivered a lovely speech during which he retraced some of the history of the club. The following is an excerpt from that speech.

For those of us who are celebrating the Bronwydd Cricket Club's twenty-first anniversary, the perception is that we have always been a successful organisation, competing in the South Wales League, fielding four teams in the South Wales Junior League, sporting an Occasionals XI and being heavily involved in the coaching and development of the game. In addition, a modern clubhouse with bar and varied new machinery complete an image of contemporary progress. Few of you will know or could even imagine the humble and sometimes bizarre beginnings of the village club.

Formed in 1978, and initially unable to identify an appropriate and reasonably flat piece of land, the original XI played away matches at locations as distant as Stackpole, Gowerton and Llanicar. But in the following year, permission was granted to play at Cymcyderi [pronounced Coomsidery] in a baptism against a Somerset touring side. The basic absence of any gang mowers pulled by a tractor to cut the grass was unimportant to an enthusiastic band of hard workers, so five electric Flymos droned the ground incessantly all day, as gradually, section by section, the field was crew-cut. Villagers had the distant impression of living inside an angry wasps' nest.

Permission had also been given to change and make tea in the derelict cowshed near the hedge; players then assumed they could shelter under the adjoining hay barn, as rain inevitably threatened in an area rightly designated the capital of wet Wales.

The following year heralded the arrival of advanced technology in the shape of an outside Elsan toilet. If you got a duck, you emptied the bucket; even the number 11 batsman tried to avoid the horrendous consequences of collecting a 'golden' duck.

The building of a new clubhouse in 1985, with a licence extending to all hours, and the advent of league cricket, heralded a movement towards normality and routine. Yet those moments of oddity continued to intrude. One sultry Saturday afternoon in June, with a contest barely half an hour old, and as the openers carefully accrued singles and the shine diminished off the ball, suddenly the whole valley was shaken by sights and sounds more reminiscent of a John Wayne Western than a sleepy west Wales village. From under the bridge, torrenting through the middle of the river, came a rampaging herd of heifers and bullocks, totally crazed by the frightening attentions of the dreaded warble fly. Taking a left-hand exit towards the cricket field, they thundered towards the play. Thirteen cricketers and an umpire headed for the safety of the pavilion, but to his eternal credit, a sole umpire stood alone and defended the holy integrity of the cricket square with some success by waving his arms and shouting, 'Shoo … shww.'

During an away game at Lampeter, two players knocking a ball around before going out to bat lost it in the hedge. After a cursory search one impatient player swung his bat into the undergrowth, managing to slice a wasps' nest in half. Wasps normally leave the game of cricket alone, apart from the occasional buzz towards a juicy teatime jam tart. But when someone demolishes their home for no apparent reason their attitude tends to change. A buzzing tornado of black anger billowed from the hedge, ignored the immediate cringing culprits, and decided to attack the citadel. The wasps hovered around the pitch where the white-clad contestants paused briefly to query the strange sound and the oscillating black crowd. The whole fielding side and the two weapon-waving batsmen and hat-swinging umpires were put to flight as they ended up in an unceremonious heap in the car park. 'Did the umpire call "dead ball"?' enquired the smug but safe scorer behind his secure glass frontage.

Touring sides soon became a feature at Bronwydd, but one year the fixture list somewhat overreached itself. On a sunny Sunday lunch time, the fixture secretary noted with some satisfaction that the Gloucestershire accents in the local pub confirmed the arrival of the Frampton on Severn cricket team for the afternoon friendly. The ground had been nicely prepared for the match, the toss was completed and the visitors were to bat first. As our opening bowler prepared to bowl, a fielder remarked, 'There's a minibus pulling into the car park.'

'It's probably their non-playing members coming to watch the game,' came the reassuring reply.

'But there are 11 of them, all carrying their cricket bags,' persisted an observant fielder.

They were hurrying towards the pavilion, seeing us all out there ready to play. The fixture secretary had now retreated towards the river, realising there had been a cock-up in the scheduling of games. It is most unusual for a batsman who has just taken middle and leg in preparation to commence his innings to be asked, 'Who are you?'

The reply was both prompt and devastating. 'We're Lucas from Birmingham. Enjoyed ourselves 'ere last year. We've coom 'ere agen!'

With three teams at one venue, the only solution was to play each other in a round robin, so that we all got a game and everyone was happy.

For the record

As well as providing details of every test, first-class and one-day match played during the year, plus a huge range of other cricketing information, the cricketer's almanac, *Wisden*, publishes obituaries when anyone in the cricketing world dies. When Donald Arthur Shepherd OBE died at the age of 82, his obituary in cricket's Bible read:

He was captain of the Leeds Grammar School and played a solitary first-class match as an Oxford undergraduate. Though he was not good enough to play for the university team, he played for Yorkshire at The Parks in 1938, when Arthur Mitchell was injured, and they needed a Yorkshire-born replacement in a hurry. He was out for nought, did not bowl and did not take a catch. He did however have a second team game later that summer where he did a little better — in that match he scored a single, bowled an over but dropped a catch. He then became a civil servant in the Colonial Service.

Impaired vision

My father, Walter, who captained the 1949 New Zealand team to England, tells a story about his great friend Len Butterfield, who also played test cricket for New Zealand. Len played only once and that was against Australia in 1946, at the Basin Reserve. It was a match that Len, Dad and New Zealand would rather forget. New Zealand was bowled out for 42 and 54 to lose by an innings and 103 runs against Bill Brown's team, which included Ray Lindwall, Keith Miller, Ernie Toshack, Sid Barnes, Lindsay Hassett, Ian Johnson, Colin McCool and Don Tallon.

Dad scored six and three, and it was not a great match for Len either — he scored a pair. According to Len he got two bad decisions in that match. In both innings he was given out lbw to Bill O'Reilly when he had hit the ball. As he walked passed the umpire, H.W. (Harry) Gourlay, Len told him, 'You should get your eyes checked.' Harry turned and looked at Len, then said, 'Funny you should say that, Len. I've just made an appointment with the optician for next week.'

So here endeth Len Butterfield's test career — one match, two innings, no runs, highest score 0, average 0.00. He did bowl 13 overs, but he failed to take a wicket and conceded 24 runs.

If you think that was a tough and short introduction to test cricket, spare a thought for G.C. (Gordon) Rowe, who fared no better. He scored a pair in the same test and never played for New Zealand again.

A touch of Frost

One year I was invited to play in the annual Wellbeing Foundation charity cricket match at Chippinghurst Manor, Oxford, England, to raise money for research into the health of women and babies. Sir David Frost, the television interviewer and presenter, and Sir Victor Blank, a businessman, were the opposing captains. The match was played at the picturesque home of Sir Victor and Lady Blank, with 650 invited guests watching former test players and businessmen doing battle in the middle, and with the result that over £250,000 was raised for the charity.

The test players included Sunil Gavaskar, Mike Denness, Phil Edmonds, Mike Procter, Barry Richards and Martin Crowe. There were several knights from the business world, and other influential people, who each paid £10,000 for the privilege of playing. The 35-over match was literally called a day-knight match.

The game had its moments. Martin Crowe scored a three-ball duck and I needed to score 13 from the final three balls to win the match, but could manage only three fours to tie the game.

Comedian Rory Bremner — who does voice impersonations of British Prime Minister Tony Blair and cricket commentators Fred Trueman, Geoff Boycott, Richie Benaud and Henry Blofeld — bowled his loopy spin-type deliveries to businessman Sir Martin Sorrell. The batsman had difficulty getting his bat near the ball. Phil Edmonds, standing at slip, yelled back to the bowler, 'Hey Rory, that ball has failed to register on the speed-ball radar.' When the next delivery had been bowled, Barry Richards said, 'That ball must have gone backwards. The speed-ball radar has registered minus 6 kph.'

I bowled the first over of the match to Sunil Gavaskar, the former Indian captain, without mishap. The ball seemed to be landing in the right place. The third ball of the second over was a 'jaffa' — it seamed, bounced and Gavaskar was well beaten by pace, with the ball going through to David Frost, who was wicket-keeping. The 70-year-old, whose glasses appeared to be fogged up, somehow got his gloves to the ball, then grappled it, juggled it, and finally caught it at about groin height as his knees hit the ground. Mike Denness, the former England captain, called out, 'Well caught, skipper. That could have been four byes.'

Sir David, in his laconic and very English way, replied, 'My dear old chap, the alternative if I had missed the ball did not bear thinking about!'

A sight to behold

The annual 30-over match in which an Old World XI take on an Old Australian XI to raise funds for multiple sclerosis research is greatly enjoyed by both players and spectators. Each year guests at an official function the night before the game are invited to bid for the position of twelfth man. In 1999, for the first time, the successful bidder for the twelfth man position for the Australian team was a woman. Not surprisingly, she was both excited and nervous, wondering just what her $1250 bid might have let her in for.

With a victory firmly in the hands of the World team, the captain of the Australian team, the legendary Dougie Walters, asked the 'twelfth man' to bowl the penultimate over. She duly obliged, walking about a pace and throwing the ball to Carl Hooper, who gently pushed the ball back to her.

Meanwhile, former England bowler John Emburey, who wasn't concentrating on the game, looked up to watch the final overs. Squinting somewhat, and having difficulty focusing from the pavilion to the middle, he mistakenly assumed the bowler was the Australian fast-bowling demon Jeff Thomson, his longish blond hair looking even more sun-bleached than usual. (In 1978 Thomson was named the fastest bowler in test history after being timed at 99 mph, or 159 kph.)

'Embers' was heard to say, 'Gosh, Thommo's slowed down to a walk these days, and what's more, he's now throwing the bleeding thing!'

Dead and buried

Alfred Shaw, the Nottinghamshire and England bowler, was the first man to bowl a ball in a test match. His dying wish was to be buried 'a cricket pitch away' from his old team-mate Arthur Shrewsbury.

The request was duly honoured, but some weeks later it was found that Shaw had been buried 27 yards away from his team-mate, rather than 22 yards.

When the error was reported to the county secretary there was great consternation. Exhumation was even considered, until the secretary himself solved the problem by declaring, 'It's all right — Alfred always took a five-yard run up.'

Paddle power

During Pakistan's tour of New Zealand in 1985, our champion batsman, Martin Crowe (known to the team as Hogan), was going through a period of self-doubt. He would wake up in the morning not knowing whether he should shave or have breakfast, or what bat he should use during the match. He gave all the indications that he was likely to fail during the day.

I would say to him, 'Hogan — you will shave, you will have bacon and eggs for breakfast, and you will use your favourite bat.'

On the first morning of the second test at Eden Park in Auckland he arrived in the dressing room and taped a chart to the wall above his seat. Using my nickname, Paddles, as a reminder, and headed, 'Listen here, Hogan, this is a test match, now is the time', the chart read:

P   Pride of performance
A   Aims and application
D   Desire to do well
D   Dedication to the job
L   Be one of the lads
E   Enjoy the game
S   Success and winning

I must admit to being a little choked up as I read the words. I then watched him produce a delightful innings of 84, until he was caught off the handle of the bat at short leg, off the bowling of Abdul Qadir. For the third test at Dunedin he added 'Hogan' to his wall chart:

H   Hundreds
O   Organisation and be prepared

G   Guts

A   Aims

N   Play natural game

During that test he scored very well with 57 and 84. The transformation of Martin Crowe during the three tests was very pleasing. He went on to average 59, having scored 295 runs, and for the first time we won a series against Pakistan in New Zealand.

While all this was going on Stephen Boock, our left-arm spinner and number 11 batsman, had noticed Crowe's motivational chart. During the third test Boock was sent in as nightwatchman and survived. Next morning he arrived at the ground with his own chart, using his nickname, Boocky, as a source of inspiration.

B   Block

O   'Ook

O   On drive

C   Cut

K   Kill the …!

Y   Yahoo

Continuing his batting, Boocky was out hooking ('ooking), so Frank Cameron, the chairman of selectors and our manager, quickly deleted ''Ook' from his chart and replaced it with 'Off drive'.

Boocky averaged five for the series.

An eye on the job

Pat Carrick was the first female umpire to officiate in a men's first-class cricket match. Although she was a former New Zealand women's team representative, there was still a lot of debate about whether a woman should be placed in a man's environment. She could be subjected to abuse and slips of the tongue, and she would have to handle the pressure that would be placed on her from excessive appealing, especially in tight and tense situations.

Pat was a true Cantabrian. During one game in the early 1980s when Otago were playing Canterbury at Lancaster Park in Christchurch, Otago felt that a number of decisions were going against them. At the drinks break Warren Lees, the Otago captain and wicket-keeper, went up to Pat and asked her, 'Pat, how do you spell your name?'

'C-A-R-R-I-C-K,' said Pat.

'Just as I thought,' said Wally; 'one I [eye].'

the
characters

A True-man

Fred Trueman will go down in history as the first bowler to capture 300 test wickets and as one of the great fast bowlers of all time. He was also a wonderful character who always had a word or two to say in any situation, and this often created some amusement for his team-mates and the opposition.

Like many fast bowlers, Fred suffered from his share of dropped catches, which frustrated him greatly. After Raman Subba Row had dropped another catch, with the ball going for four runs, he apologised, saying, 'Sorry, Fred. It might have been better if I had kept my legs together.'

Fred, quick as a flash, responded, 'Aye lad, it's a pity your mother didn't!'

'Smokin' Bill Wyman

The rock star Bill Wyman, of the Rolling Stones, is often coaxed into playing charity cricket matches for the Bunbury XI. In one year every game he played in was affected by rain, but he would turn out to demonstrate his skills and support various causes. David English, a former actor and raconteur, is the genius behind the Bunburys, and organises ex-players and celebrities to travel around England and play matches on Sunday afternoons in support of cricket beneficiaries and charities.

Bill 'Benson and Hedges' Wyman, a left-handed batsman, is the only man to take a televised hat-trick at the Oval — taking soccer star Gary Lineker, news presenter Trevor McDonald, and commentator Charles Colville live on Sky Sports. He also gets through 40 fags a match.

In his own words, Bill has fond memories of some of the games he has played. 'Playing against Norma Major's XI, I caught out former England captain Brian Close — then 66 — one-handed off the bowling of former soccer star Ian Wright. That in itself was a major miracle, but I did it without disturbing the ash from my fag, which was drenched from the rain, in the other hand.

'On another occasion, I was fielding in the slips in the rain with Dennis Lillee, who was gobsmacked to see Eric Clapton and myself smoking during play. Eric was dressed in his yellow oilskins, looking as though he had just stepped off a Norwegian whaling boat, and was letting every ball that came near him pass by for four runs, ensuring that his fingers were still intact for his next guitar performance.'

It's all in a name

Ian Healy, the former Australian wicket-keeper and world record holder for most test dismissals, had his testimonial cricket match at the Gabba on 21 December 2000. Players from all round the world came to honour this great achiever, including Graham Gooch from England, Desmond Haynes, Jeff Dujon, Sir Vivian Richards and Courtney Walsh from the West Indies, Brian McMillan and Kepler Wessels from South Africa, and Abdul Qadir from Pakistan.

Some of the current Australian test team, including Michael Slater, Mark Waugh, Andy Bichel and Shane Warne, had joined former greats Allan Border, David Boon, Craig McDermott and Merv Hughes to convincingly beat the World team in front of 16,000 spectators.

'Heals' was telling the story of how he had contacted and approached the players about the match. To contact Abdul Qadir, the former Pakistani leg spinner, he first had to speak to someone from the Pakistan Board of Control to get his phone number. Having done this, Heals rang Abdul.

'Abdul,' he said. 'Ian Healy speaking from Australia. How are you?'

'Fine,' was the reply.

'How are the balls coming out of your fingers?'

'Pardon?'

'Are you playing and getting a few wickets?'

'I do not understand.'

'Is that Abdul Qadir, the cricketer?'

'No. This is Doctor Abdul Qadir, nuclear physicist.'

Apparently, the name Abdul Qadir is quite common in Pakistan.

Heal's Achilles

During his testimonial luncheon Ian Healy told how he had had two embarrassing moments on the cricket field. Ian was never one to worry about statistics and records, so he says. He preferred to play the game and let the records look after themselves.

His first embarrassing moment came when he was batting with his captain, Allan Border, against New Zealand at Lancaster Park, Christchurch, in the early 1990s. There had been a lot of hype and speculation in the media about when Allan Border would create batting history, which Ian seemed to be unaware of.

At one point in the match A.B. pushed the ball into the covers then ran down the pitch punching his fists into the air. 'That's it,' he said jubilantly.

'That's what?' said Heals.

'That's the record.'

'What record?' said Heals.

'The most runs scored by a batsman in test history,' said his captain.

Allan Border had just eclipsed the world record held by India's Sunil Gavaskar by scoring 10,122 test runs.

The second embarrassing occasion for Heals was when New Zealand was playing Australia at Eden Park in 1990. It was a one-day match and New Zealand was in trouble. Fortunately, I was able to score a few runs to make us more competitive than had seemed likely a little earlier in the day.

When I was eventually dismissed for 79, my highest one-day score, I raised my bat to the crowd, did a few circles to acknowledge their applause, and raised my bat again. I removed my hat and bowed and thanked the crowd for their support, then walked slowly towards the players' tunnel and the dressing room.

While all this was going on the Australians were in a huddle congratulating each other on getting another wicket. Heals said, 'Look at that silly bugger waving to the crowd. He's making an idiot of himself. Hurry up and get off the field you … fool!'

One of Heals' team-mates quietly said to him, 'It's his last game for New Zealand,' at which Heals admitted to feeling about two feet high and not being able to find a hole big enough to hide in.

The Bedser twins

Sir Alec and Eric Bedser, who are twin brothers, are the closest of friends. They look alike, they dress alike, they talk alike, they think alike, they live together and neither has ever married. They became profes-sional cricketers together, served in the Second World War together, and were the core members of a great Surrey cricket team during the 1950s. Alec played test cricket for England and went on to capture 236 test wickets at 24.89.

Both men were invited to come to New Zealand for a cricket function in 2000. At that time they were in their eighties. When asked if people sometimes got them confused, Sir Alec replied, 'Not really.' He thought for a minute, then went on, 'Yes, there was that time when Frank Woolley got us confused.' (Woolley was one of the game's greatest all-rounders, with nearly 59,000 first-class runs, including 145 centuries and 2068 wickets at 19.85.)

'We were playing a charity match at the end of the war, Old England versus Surrey,' Sir Alec continued. 'There were a lot of big names there, including Percy Fender, Patsy Hendren and Andy Sandham. Sir Jack Hobbs umpired. I was bowling to Woolley, who was in his fifties by then, but he was still a magnificent player. He kept driving me over mid-off like he was teeing off at golf.

'In one over, I bowled the first three balls at normal pace. Then Eric, who was fielding at mid-on, bowled the last three balls with his offspin. At the end of the over Woolley, who had no idea who we were, turned to our wicket-keeper, George Mobey, and said, "This fellow Bedser has a good change of pace." '

Pressure? What pressure?

After representing England with great distinction Sir Alec Bedser was an England selector for two decades, and for a time the England team manager. He had fun as a selector, dropping Geoff Boycott and Ken Barrington for batting selfishly. He also had to deal with Boycott's self-imposed exile from the game, and the repercussions from the Kerry Packer attack on the cricket establishment.

During an interview about his life in cricket Sir Alec commented, 'I enjoyed selecting. Not everyone does. Peter May didn't, and I don't think Ted Dexter did either. But I never worried.

'Look, it's only a game. As Keith Miller used to say, "Pressure? There is no pressure in cricket. Pressure is when you have a Messerschmitt up your arse." '

Who will be the lucky one today?

Fred Trueman was a great exponent of the art of gamesmanship, and he inspired fear in the hearts of many a young professional who was trying to make his way in the game. He would frequently walk into the opposition dressing room, look around at the players and say, 'Good morning, lads. I need nine more wickets to reach my 100 for the season. I suggest you look around between yourselves to see who will be the lucky one I don't get today.'

Anyone can succeed!

Merv Hughes, the burly, mustachioed Australian and Victorian fast bowler, was one of the great characters of cricket in recent years. He was involved in many controversial moments both on and off the field, including spitting at batsmen, giving verbal abuse and indulging in byplay with the crowds. He captured 212 test wickets for his country, and was recognised as a great Australian with the heart of a lion, always giving 100 percent. He had a huge following in Australia.

At Ian Healy's testimonial luncheon, at which Merv was present, Heals paid tribute to his cricketing friends who had travelled from afar to play in his testimonial match at the Gabba. In thanking Merv for his support, he said, 'Merv Hughes is a living example to young people of someone who can succeed when they haven't got a brain.'

Those at the luncheon relished the humour as a wry smile appeared on Merv's face.

Just more tripe

Arthur Mailey was a right-arm leg spin bowler who played for Australia in the 1920s, touring both England and South Africa. He played 21 tests and captured 99 wickets, at an average of 33.91. He was a big spinner of the ball but at times he suffered from poor line and length, which made him an inconsistent performer.

He was also a clever cartoonist and oil painter, and he had great wit. When he retired from the game he wrote cricketing articles and later became a butcher. On the door of his shop he had a sign that read: 'I used to bowl tripe, then I wrote it and now I sell it.'

'The Cat'

Philip Tufnell, the Middlesex and England left-arm orthodox spin bowler, was nicknamed 'The Cat'. The reason was not, as you might imagine, his feline agility and pace in the field, nor his ability to pounce on the ball and return it to the keeper all in one movement. His team-mates gave him the name because in the field he had a habit of taking a 'catnap' and misfielding or dropping an easy catch.

Australian crowds heckled 'Tuffers' every time the ball went his way. When he misfielded the ball or dropped a catch they would all chorus in unison, 'Philip Tufnell's school of fielding.'

A close encounter

Australia's dynamic fast bowling duo of Dennis Lillee and Jeff Thomson formed one of the most lethal bowling combinations of all time. They terrorised individual batsmen and teams during the 1970s and 1980s.

The pair developed a great friendship and rivalry both on and off the field. After one match, a reporter asked Dennis, 'What would you do if you had only 30 minutes to live?'

'I'd make love to the first thing that moved,' Dennis replied.

When Thommo was asked the same question he responded, 'I'm not moving for 30 minutes.'

Down the gurgler

Michael Slater, the Australian opening batsman, waited a long time for the opportunity to play for his country. The swashbuckling cricketer had a proven first-class record, and when he was selected many people thought he would make an immediate impact on the game, which he did. However, he had a reputation among his team-mates for showing extreme disappointment and frustration when he was dismissed, especially with a low score. He would berate himself and throw his gear around, and his fellow players would avoid him until he had mellowed.

In a test match at the beautiful Adelaide Oval Slats was dismissed for 0 in the first innings and the same old frustration was exhibited again. In the second innings he was dismissed for two and the other players waited in expectation of the usual performance, vacating the dressing room and sitting in the players' viewing room waiting for a tirade of abuse. For a few minutes no noise came from the dressing room, but the players were still expectant. Ten minutes passed and there was still no noise. In relief, his team-mates thought that he must at last have come to terms with his anger and frustration. Slats eventually appeared in the players' viewing room, where he sat quietly in his chair and watched the game.

At the fall of another Australian wicket Mark Waugh went down to pad up and have the usual nervous toilet visit. He quickly returned to the viewing area, however, where he advised the team that Slats' pads, bat, gloves and box had been jammed down the only toilet bowl in the dressing room!

A horney one!

In a letter to the editor of the *Sunday Star-Times* Ivan Williams wrote that he was intrigued at how many commentators referred to members of New Zealand's Black Caps by their nicknames, such as 'Cairnsy' (Chris Cairns), 'Flem' (Stephen Fleming), 'Nashie' (Dion Nash) and 'Youngie' (Bryan Young). He went on, 'But I have yet to hear them refer to Matt [Matthew Horne] as "Horney"!'

Light refreshments!

Harold 'Dickie' Bird and Barrie Meyer umpired in the 1978 test between New Zealand and England. It was the first time umpires had been allowed to use light meters to assess whether conditions were good enough for play to continue. When the meter fell below a certain level on the gauge, the umpires would offer the light to the batsmen and all the players would leave the field of play.

Later Dickie recalled a test match between Australia and England at Old Trafford in the early 1980s when, 'We all trooped off the field of play, and one Lancashire member, who appeared to have had just a little too much liquid refreshment, shouted, "You are off again, Bird, bringing them off again as usual. Sun's shining; light's perfect. What's the problem this time, Bird?"

'No problem at all, sir,' Dickie replied. 'It's lunch.'

Perceptions!

Ray Illingworth, the England and Leicestershire captain, was an inspirational man who had an impressive record as captain. He had the ability to make the right decision and get the desired result, although some people think there is always an element of luck when it comes to captaincy.

In one particular match, when Leicestershire were in a lot of trouble, Illy decided to bring on the off-spinner Jack Birkenshaw to bowl. Birky went on to capture 4/6 in an inspired spell of bowling, enabling Leicestershire to win the match. The headlines in the following morning's paper read: 'Wily old fox does it again'.

'Wily old fox?' Birky spluttered as we sat in the pub the next day. 'Shall I tell you what the wily old fox said? "Lob 'em up, Jack — t'game's boogered." '

A wake-up call

Stephen Boock tells a story about the Auckland Cricket Association secretary and first-class umpire Graham Cowan. Otago were playing Auckland at Eden Park, and Graham was one of the umpires. To Otago, some of the decisions appeared to favour the home side, Auckland — there were several caught behind and lbw decisions going against the away team.

After 30 minutes of play Boocky went up to Graham at the end of an over and said, 'Graham. As players, we get up at 7 a.m., have breakfast at 7.30, leave the hotel for the ground at 9 a.m., we practise from 9.15 until 10 a.m., and play starts at 10.30 a.m. It would be nice to think that by 11 a.m. you would be awake.'

growing up
with
the game

A Hogg's tale

Australian Rodney Hogg was a magnificent fast bowler during the late 1970s and early 1980s. His batting was a different story, however. He batted at number 11 and scored only a few runs, averaging just 9.75 in test cricket.

On one occasion Australia was playing the West Indies at the WACA ground in Perth, reputedly the fastest and bounciest pitch in the world. Hoggy had to face the awesome pace-bowling attack of Andy Roberts, Michael Holding, Colin Croft and the 'Big Bird', Joel Garner, a daunting experience.

He faced a few deliveries without laying bat on any of them. After being hit twice on the body he decided the best way to play this sort of bowling was to give himself some room outside the leg stump, although the square umpire suggested it would be a good idea to get off his foot and get closer to the stumps to face the next delivery. A couple of balls later the wickets were shattered and Hoggy trudged back to the pavilion somewhat disconsolately. He immediately got on the phone and called his wife. 'Did you video the test like I asked you to do?' he said.

'Yes, I did,' she responded.

'All of it?' asked Hoggy.

'Yes.'

'Did you get my innings on video?'

'Yes, I got it all.'

'Well erase the last bit,' said Hoggy. 'I don't want my son growing up thinking I was a coward.'

A late punishment

As a youngster I was always very keen on the game of cricket. I played at all levels of the game, but the most important part was the training I received at school, where I learnt some of the basic disciplines that were so important in my future development. I enjoyed my years at Christchurch Boys' High School, and think of it as a time to remember.

I recall arriving late one day for a school First XI practice during the holidays. The coach, Ray Thomson, was furious.

'Why were you late for practice, Richard?'

'I was late when I started from home, sir.'

'Why didn't you leave earlier?'

'Because I was too late to start earlier, sir.'

My comments may have raised a little smile from Coach Thomson, but he had the last say. I was made twelfth man for the next match — and was never late again.

Too much pace

Playing for the Christchurch Boys' High School First XI was always a special occasion for me. It engendered a sense of great pride, and among our peers it was a status symbol to have the blue school sports blazer with 'First XI Cricket 1967, 1968, 1969' embroidered in gold on the pocket.

Our coach, Ray Thomson, who was the head of the physical education department at CBHS, had been a prominent basketball player and administrator in Christchurch. He would have been the first to admit that he knew little about cricket, but no one could complain about his enthusiasm for the game and for the players. He also made sure the players didn't get too carried away with their ability or form.

On one occasion Ray said to me, 'You are bowling like lightning today, Richard.'

'You mean I was bowling fast, sir?' I responded.

'No, you never seem to strike in the same place twice.'

I knew then that I had to start working a lot more on my accuracy, rather than trying to bowl too fast.

An impasse

Every year Ray Thomson, the coach at Christchurch Boys' High, had the same problem, with at least half the First XI players leaving school. Each year he would have to find new players from the Second and Third XI to fill the shoes of the experienced players who had moved on.

One day when he was trying to solve this problem Ray asked a promising new player, 'What are you like as a wicket-keeper?'

'Passable,' came the reply from the 16-year-old.

'That's no good,' said Ray. 'We already have a player like that. We need one that's impassable!'

Big mouth

Spectators who heckle cricketers cause a lot of frustration for the players, who are usually trying to do their best and want to be successful. It is the nature of the game that there will always be highs and lows. I once saw an old film of the 1949 New Zealand team on their successful tour of England, which my father, Walter, captained. The film showed Dad dropping a very easy catch, at which the commentator said, 'Oh, butterfingers Hadlee!'

When I asked Dad if he remembered the incident he replied, 'Yes I do. While the commentator said, "Butterfingers Hadlee," there was a spectator who said, "Pathetic butterfingers. I could have caught that with my mouth." '

'What did you say?' I asked him.

'I grinned,' said Dad. 'I looked over at the bloke and I said, "Mate, if I had a mouth as big as yours, I could have too."'

An average score

Jeff Crowe, the former New Zealand captain, served his country well as a batsman for a number of years, averaging about 26 in tests. At one point, when 'Chopper' was going through a bit of a lean period and scoring few runs, he was also doing some coaching.

During one session he asked a youngster whether he batted or bowled. The lad responded by saying that he batted.

'What's your batting average for the season?' asked Chopper.

'About two,' replied the youngster.

'Just like mine,' said Jeff.

A day to remember

An unnamed cricketer's wife was in full flow, saying to her husband, 'All you think about is cricket, cricket and more cricket. I bet you couldn't tell me what day we were married!'

'Yes I could,' replied her husband. 'It was the day Richard Hadlee took 9/52 against the Australians at the Gabba — 15 December 1985.'

Brothers in arms

In the history of the game of cricket there are several sets of brothers who have played together and gone on to represent their countries. Hedley and Geoff Howarth, Brendon and John Bracewell, Martin and Jeff Crowe, and my brothers Dayle, Barry and I all represented New Zealand. In Australia the Chappell brothers — Ian, Greg and Trevor — represented the green and gold, while Sadiq and Mushtaq Mohammad played for Pakistan.

One of the greatest family names associated with cricket, however, is Grace. The most famous of the Grace brothers was the legendary 'grandfather of cricket', Dr W.G. (William Gilbert) Grace. He scored over 55,000 first-class runs, including 126 centuries, captured nearly 3000 first-class wickets, and played in 22 test matches for England. His brother Dr Edward Mills Grace scored over 10,000 first-class runs and captured 305 first-class wickets, while a second brother (one of five), George Frederick Grace, scored nearly 7000 first-class runs and captured 328 first-class wickets.

Fred, as he was known, would have to be one of the unluckiest cricketing brothers. He played with W.G. and Edward in the first test ever. This took place between England and Australia in 1880. Fred caught George Bonner off a skyer, but not before the batsman had run three. Fred then went on to score the first pair ever to be recorded in test history. Two weeks later, he slept in a damp bed while travelling in a train to Southampton to play in a county match. He caught a cold and died three days later. He was only 30 years old.

touring

A close call

During the second test at Lord's in July 1999, New Zealand were heading for victory with a magnificent team performance. Fast bowler Andrew Caddick, a New Zealander who had decided to qualify and play for England, was batting when he turned for three runs and the wickets were broken at the bowler's end by Nathan Astle. There was an appeal for a run-out decision that was always going to be a close call.

Vic Marks, the former Somerset and England all-rounder, was in the radio commentary box with Christopher Martin Jenkins. Vic said, 'The umpires have referred the decision to the third umpire and it will be a hairline decision for all the players in the middle.'

C.M.J. responded, 'That's an interesting way of putting it, Victor. Daryl Hair has returned to Australia. It will be Nigel Plews [who is bald] who will be asked to make the decision from the television box.'

For the record, Caddick was run out by a few millimetres and New Zealand eventually went on to win their first ever test match at Lord's after 13 tests and 60 years of trying.

They also went on to win the series 2–1, becoming New Zealand's most successful touring team to England.

Calling a wide!

Jock Edwards, the short and rather rotund Nelson, Central Districts and New Zealand wicket-keeper batsman, sometimes stood at first slip when he wasn't keeping wickets.

On the tour of England in 1978 Jock was the wicket-keeper for the first two tests before Bruce Edgar took over in the third and final test at Lord's. Unfortunately, Jock didn't have a happy tour with the gloves or with the bat. His technique and perhaps his lack of agility and fitness had caught up with him, but his jovial personality never changed and he added to the dressing room team morale.

In one of the first-class tour matches Jock played as a specialist batsman and when we fielded he stood at first slip. I was bowling at the time, and I said to Mark Burgess, the captain, 'Do you think Jock is a bit wide at slip?'

'Gosh!' said Burge. 'If he was any wider, he'd explode.'

An international domestic

I tend to spend quite a lot of time in Auckland doing promotional work, which means flying from Christchurch to Auckland, picking up a taxi from Auckland airport to the city centre, taking a taxi back to the airport and flying home.

On one occasion I had completed my work in Auckland so I hailed a taxi to take me to the airport. I sat in the back seat and the Indian driver appeared to recognise me, so I started to feel important and respected. He was looking in his rear-vision mirror and smiling. I thought he would start talking to me because I know Indians love their cricket, and often know a lot about the players and about the history of the game. In fact, many Indians are fanatical about the subject.

The taxi driver said to me, 'Where are you going, sir?'

Thinking I could impress him further, I said, 'Actually, I'm off to Singapore to speak at a function with Sean Fitzpatrick, the former All Black captain.'

'Oh no, sir!' he said. 'I mean are you going to the domestic terminal or the international terminal?'

Time to party

During a tour of the West Indies in 1985 the New Zealand team were asked to attend a lot of functions, including some parties for local hero Clive Lloyd, who was having a benefit season. The cricket on the field of play was hard work, although we were competitive, drawing the first and second tests but losing the four-match series 2–0. We then went on to lose the one-day series 5–0.

We were only too happy to enjoy some socialising from time to time to take our minds off the beatings we were receiving, and the feared fast bowling attack of Andy Roberts, Michael Holding, Joel Garner, Malcolm Marshall and Winston Davis. Ken Rutherford had scored just 11 runs in seven test innings, and Jeremy Coney had his arm broken in the fourth test at Jamaica, so it was tough going for everyone.

When we travelled to Guyana, the home of Clive Lloyd, we learnt that the country was under a dictatorship and we would have to stay in the hotel in the evenings for security reasons. The thought of hotel meals for the next ten nights was not very appealing. In fact, it looked as if we were going to find life very boring in that part of the world.

We were happy to learn that Clive had organised several functions, which we were invited to attend. At one function we enjoyed a tasty meal — the meat tasted a little like lamb, but with a difference. When I asked what it was I was told, 'Roast laba.'

'What is roast laba?' I asked.

'Rodent,' came the reply.

We had just eaten roasted rat, which wasn't a comforting thought at the time.

The next night Clive invited us to another function, asking, 'Do any of you Kiwis want to come to a letterbox party?'

We were naturally curious, and asked Clive what a letterbox party was. Quick as a flash he responded, 'All male.'

At least the meal was better at that party. Chicken was always going to be more appealing than rat.

The name game

In recent times the International Cricket Council (ICC) has been very active in trying to develop interest in the game in countries where cricket needs a boost. In 2000 I was appointed one of 24 cricket ambassadors who visited countries in the East Asia Pacific region, which includes China, Japan, Fiji, Samoa, Hong Kong, Malaysia, Indonesia and Papua New Guinea.

On one occasion I spoke at a fundraising dinner in Jakarta where $25,000 was raised for their development fund. During the same visit I also attended, as an observer, the inaugural meeting of the unification of the Jakarta Cricket Association and the Bali Cricket Association, to form the Indonesian Cricket Foundation.

In most of the established countries that play cricket many members of the public are very well-informed about the game and I am often recognised in the street or at airports, which is a great compliment. On my return home from Jakarta to Christchurch I sat next to an American on the Jakarta–Singapore leg of the journey. Without introducing ourselves, we started to chat.

'Where are you going?' I enquired.

'Tel Aviv,' the American responded.

'What sort of work do you do?' I continued.

'I sell to governments,' was his reply.

My initial reaction was that he was an arms dealer, and so I changed the subject as quickly as I could. Fortunately he made it a little easier by asking me where I had been and what I did. When I told him I had been to Jakarta to speak at a cricket dinner, sport became very much the subject. We started talking about tennis, soccer, ice hockey and American football, and famous names were mentioned such as Pete Sampras, Pele, Wayne Gretzsky and 'The Refrigerator' Mr Perry. It was almost as if we were trying to impress each other by mentioning as many names as we could in each sport. The subject of cricket was soon raised and I thought that I would win some points here. The American started well, however, saying, 'There is a legendary fellow from Australia who batted like our baseball legend, Babe Ruth.'

'Sir Donald Bradman,' I said.

'Yeah, that's him. And there is a great player from India who is in the news at present. He has a world record or something.'

'You're thinking of Kapil Dev, the bowler. The West Indian fast bowler Courtney Walsh currently has the world record for most test wickets in the history of the game,' I said.

'Yeah. Kapil Dev, that's him.'

I continued the questioning. 'Have you heard of Dennis Lillee?'

'Yeah, I have. He did some pitching, didn't he?'

'He was a great fast bowler from Australia,' I said. 'What about Ian Botham. Have you heard of him?'

'He used to bat and bowl a bit, didn't he?' he responded.

'Yes, he was a great all-rounder from England,' I said. 'What about Imran Khan? Have you heard of him?'

'He was an all-rounder from Pakistan.'

I thought the timing was right to ask the obvious question. 'Have you heard of Richard Hadlee?'

'No. What did he do?'

'Oh,' I said. 'He used to bowl and bat a bit for New Zealand between 1972 and 1990 and had the world record for most test wickets before Kapil Dev took over the mantle.'

'No. Never heard of him,' the American confirmed.

As the plane touched down in Singapore we shook hands. 'If you're ever in Baltimore, look me up,' he said. 'The name is Joe Windberg. You can find me in the phone book.'

'OK. I'll do that. Thanks very much,' I replied. 'And if you are ever in Christchurch, look me up as well. The name is Dick Hadle.'

Best of luck today, sir

When cricket teams tour overseas some young players are always included in the squad to gain valuable experience. Young players are always keen to play as many games as possible so they can impress the selectors, but the reality is that they do not play many games at all. Usually there is a young batsman, a reserve wicket-keeper, a spinner and perhaps one fast bowler, all selected so they can learn their trade.

When Pakistan toured New Zealand in 1972/73 they had a young fast bowler called Sikander Bakht with them. He wasn't having a happy tour; his main role was being twelfth man and doing jobs for his team-mates.

The test at Wellington's Basin Reserve was my debut test, and I walked out to the wicket feeling somewhat apprehensive, as I was about to face the fast bowling of Sarfraz Nawaz and Saleem Altaf.

Zaheer Abbas had temporarily left the field with a headache, and Sikander was on the field fielding at third man. As I passed him he said, 'Good afternoon, Mr Hadlee sir. I am very much hoping that you have a very successful day with the bat today and score many, many runs.'

I went on to score 46, got dropped for the next two tests, and Sikander didn't play in another match during the tour.

Getting a bagging when you don't succeed

The England cricket team came in for severe bagging during the 1990s, especially during the 1998/99 Ashes tour of Australia. They drew the first test, but lost the next two, meaning they couldn't regain the famous Ashes. While they won the fourth test, they lost the last test narrowly to lose the series 3/1. That was when the jokes started.

'Who is the best English batsman on the current tour?'
Answer: Sky commentator Ian Botham.

'What is the height of great optimism?'
Answer: An English batsman going out to bat with suncream on his nose.

'What would Australia's fast bowler and number 11 batsman be if he was an Englishman?'
Answer: An all-rounder.

'Why is Darren Gough the unluckiest bowler on tour?'
Answer: Because he was born in England.

'What is the main function of the England coach?'

Answer: To transport the team from the hotel to the ground.

'What is England's version of a hat-trick?'

Answer: Three runs in three balls.

'Why don't English fielders need pre-tour travel injections?'

Answer: Because they never catch anything.

'What is England's version of lbw?'

Answer: Lost, walloped, beaten.

'What do you call an Englishman with a 100 against his name?'

Answer: A bowler.

Consternation!

Australia's Greg Matthews was a talented all-rounder, but he had an unusual personality that frustrated many of the opposition. People often described him as different, so much so, they said, 'that he is the only cricketer to suffer from constipation in India' — a tough goal for any player to achieve!

For some players who have travelled on the subcontinent, sitting on the loo waiting for a lump to come was a great highlight. For others, shitting through the eye of a needle was a possibility. The hardest thing, however, was trying to find a needle!

the commentators and the media

Out in the cold

Commentators can find themselves in embarrassing situations when developing a thought or theme, or describing a piece of play, and find they need to bail out. One television commentator was on air just after a commercial break when the cameras panned in on Bryan Young.

'Welcome back to the Basin Reserve here in Wellington,' he started promisingly, 'where conditions are very cold indeed. There is Bryan Young, standing at first slip, wearing two sweaters, putting his hands in his pockets to keep warm between balls.'

A Crowe's call

A quote in one of New Zealand's Sunday newspapers recalled a statement made by Martin Crowe, the former New Zealand batsman and now a radio and television commentator, who had found a new way of stating the obvious during a one-day match at Eden Park: 'This one is going to go all the way to the finish.'

Even the best get it wrong

Iain Gallaway was known as one of New Zealand's best cricket and rugby radio commentators. He had a certain type of voice and charm that made for easy listening. He was an avid Otago supporter, and when he was in the commentary box at Carisbrook in Dunedin his opening lines would be, 'Welcome to Carisbrook, where there is not a cloud in the sky.' Whether it was raining or not, Iain was proud of the Otago weather and playing conditions. When he wrote his autobiography it was appropriately titled *Not a Cloud in the Sky*.

Iain was always very precise about what he wanted to say and when, and he had immaculate diction. However, like all commentators he sometimes slipped up. On one memorable day he began in his usual fashion, 'Welcome back to Carisbrook, where there is not a cloud in the sky.' He then went on, 'That was a lovely shot by Richard Hoskin, who has driven that ball through the covers for four. What a magnificent shot, and the cloud craps.'

I'm sure the *crowd clapped* when they heard that comment on the radio!

A mathematical brain

Another commentator went on to say, 'So the required runs needed are 67 from 11 overs and it doesn't take a calculator to tell us that the run rate is 6.0909 recurring.'

A crappy call

A former Australian player who went on to become a radio commentator got caught short on air when describing a dropped catch in a test match. With a simplicity that no one could argue with, he said, 'Shit, he's missed it.'

Distinguishing features

Speaking at a function in Tauranga, Iain Gallaway took great delight in telling the audience that commentators need to have a method of distinguishing the players from one another, especially new or foreign players with whom they are not familiar. It can be difficult to differentiate between players who are a hundred metres away from the commentary box. The trick, he said, is to watch the team practice on the morning of the match from close quarters, and to try to note the players' distinguishing features.

On the scorecard Iain would write notes against the players' names, so that when he was on air and sometimes looking through the binoculars he could correctly identify them. During Sri Lanka's 1988/89 tour of New Zealand he made the following observations:

Ravi Ratnayake	pigeon-toed
Jayawanda Warnawera	big ears
Roshan Mahanama	no chin
Asanka Gurusinha	droopy moustache
Arjuna Ranatunga	rotund
Aravinda De Silva	short and stocky
Ranjan Madugalle	smiley
Brendon Kuruppu	tall and thin
Graham Labrooy	whitish colour
Guy de Alwis	tall and well-built (wicket-keeper)
Rumesh Ratnayake	large white eyes

Spending up

During the first test between England and South Africa at Edgbaston, Birmingham, in 1998, Darren Gough broke his finger while batting. When England fielded, the specialist fielder took Gough's place and 19-year-old Ben Spendlove from Derbyshire had the honour of taking the field.

He excelled himself when he held onto two catches from fellow Derbyshire player and captain Dominic Cork at bat-pad.

Tony Lewis, the former England captain and now a television commentator, was having some difficulty coming to terms with the youngster's name.

'Ben Spendlove is not an easy name to remember,' he said. 'I'll have to think of a little phrase to remind me of the name. When I get home from work, I'll have to say to my wife, "Hi, sweetheart. Did you have a good day? How much did you spend, luv?"'

Did it really rain?

One commentator was heard to say, 'There has been some heavy rain here today at Jade Stadium, Lancaster Park, Christchurch — fortunately it didn't touch the ground.'

Resurrecting the corpse

During the 1990s England's constant string of batting failures led to a lot of negative comments in the media, and the team was publicly criticised by a number of former players. When the team started to achieve some positive results, the commentators had their own ways of getting the point across.

England's Trevor Bailey, describing some good English batting during a test match, was inspired to say, 'Alan Lamb and David Gower have resurrected the situation. We owe a lot of gratitude to both players, who have breathed some life into a corpse that had nearly expired.'

Shooting from the hip

Brian Johnstone, an Englishman, was one of the best cricket commentators to describe the game. Like all commentators, he occasionally got his words tangled. During one game he got a little tied up as he described a player's crouching position in the slips area: 'He looks as though he is shitting, I mean sitting, on his shooting stick without the shooting stick.'

Dressed in whites

England's John Arlott, who was sometimes referred to as the doyen of commentators, also had some different ways of getting the point across to his listeners. For example, 'It is rather suitable that umpires should dress like dentists, since one of their tasks is to draw stumps.'

The charming snakes!

For 12 years cricket between India and Pakistan was in limbo because of political strife between the two countries. In 1999 it was decided the two countries should resume cricket contests, with a test series being staged in India. There was some concern that the tour might be disrupted, because radical groups had already dug up a pitch and promised to prevent the series taking place, so the local authorities needed to make sure security was tight.

A report in India's *Pioneer* newspaper noted that snake charmers would be among the thousands of security personnel at the second test in New Delhi. The report stated:

The services of snake charmers have been requested by New Delhi police, in view of threats by the radical right wing Hindu Shiv Sena Party to let loose snakes in the stadium. Sena leader Bal Thackeray has since withdrawn the protest against the resumption of cricketing ties between the two South Asian neighbours after a gap of 12 years, but the authorities are taking no chances.

Just as well there are no snakes in New Zealand.

An accurate call

Spectators can also be extremely vocal on occasion. During one game a spectator who was becoming increasingly frustrated with a bowler who was being hit for plenty of runs expressed his displeasure with devastating sarcasm.

'That player is a great bowler. He is so accurate — every time he bowls the ball, he finds the middle of the bat.'

Sorry, sir

An article in Christchurch's *Press* newspaper headed 'Knight of the round ball' read:

A *Press* reader's daughter holidaying in India was reminded of the country's fanaticism for cricket last month. A shopkeeper asked her where she came from, to which she replied, 'New Zealand.' The man's eyes lit up and he said, 'Ah, Martin Crowe.'

In the next shop, the same question received the same response, with the woman adding: 'Yes, I come from the same town as Richard Hadlee.' The shopkeeper studied the woman for a moment and said reproachfully, 'Sir Richard Hadlee.'

For the benefit of all

In a boring, drawn-out cricket match with few spectators and no interest in the game, the ground announcer made the following statement: 'For the benefit of the players in the middle, here are the names of the spectators.'

All I want for Christmas is ...

Karen Nimmo, a reporter with the *Sunday News* newspaper, wrote a Christmas article in December 1998 in which she listed sporting requests from various sporting personalities.

Dear Clausey
I am after 11 presents this year. They are the presents you didn't give me last year. I want two opening batsmen, one solid middle-order batsman, some bowlers, preferably two pace bowlers, a medium pacer, a spinner, and a wicket-keeper who can stop and catch the ball and score some runs.
Thanks.
Cheers
Steve Rixon
(New Zealand cricket coach and national selector)

It appears the presents arrived, because after inconsistent performances in 1997/98, the New Zealand team played admirably against
India and South Africa during the 1998/99 season. New Zealand won the
test series 1–0 and squared the one-day series 2–2 against India. They
lost the test series 1–0 to South Africa but were more competitive in the
one-day series, losing 3–2.

Another letter to Santa read:

> Dear Santa
> I am looking for a job. I have done all the hard yards and now I
> am on the dole queue. They took the Warriors coaching job from
> me and now I have got to wait until January to see whether I
> have got the Kiwi job.
>
> If you are looking to recruit more Santas for this year, I look
> great in red.
> Frank Endacott
> (Rugby league coach)

Frank Endacott had been sacked by the new owners of the Warriors, but
later got the coaching job of the Kiwi rugby league team.

A dual role

As part of their role in promoting cricket, the Bank of New Zealand
produced a series of television commercials involving two groundsmen.
Don Langridge played the older and more experienced groundsman,
while Tim Sprite was the younger and less competent of the two, keen
to make an impression and eventually take over from Don.

During the 1998 season BNZ decided it was time to freshen up the commercials by having me appear as the Bank of New Zealand ambassador in several different situations. It is interesting when you read the scripts and practise the lines, then see how they change when filming takes place — the finished product is sometimes very different from the original script.

In one commercial, titled 'BNZ Hospitality', Don and Tim have smartened themselves up by wearing jackets and ties and are attending a hospitality luncheon with the bank's guests. The filming starts off with the pair sampling some wine and chatting to one another. I am standing in the background talking to some other guests when I overhear part of their conversation.

A waiter offers Tim a glass of wine, saying, 'Try this one, sir; I think you will like the grassy smells in this wine.'

Don strolls up to Tim as he is sniffing the wine, and Tim says, 'I think this wine smells of rye grass.'

'Yes,' says Don, 'a mixture of rye, southern bent grass, coarse-leaf Bermuda — badly in need of mowing and rolling if you ask me.'

'An insy winsy bouquet of paspalum creeping into it,' Tim adds.

'And I think it will start taking some spin on the third day,' responds Don.

I am now standing behind as Tim, whose knowledge of cricket is pretty limited, says questioningly, 'Paspalum, Paspalum … Didn't he play for Pakistan?'

'India,' I say.

Tim looks round, surprised to see me there, then turns to Don and says confidently, 'That's Ewen Chatfield!'

The original script did not have my comment about India, and Tim said my name instead of 'Ewen Chatfield'. But we all agreed the ad lib worked well.

In another scene at the Basin Reserve in Wellington, a commercial with a 'windy' theme was filmed. With the help of a big petrol-operated fan to provide additional wind to create the effect of a gale, the scene was set. As it turned out, there was almost enough natural wind at the ground, which is typical of Wellington.

Tim is standing on the embankment with a device like a propeller in his hand to indicate how strong the wind is. The device is going like the clappers when Don strolls up behind Tim and asks, 'What's that?'

'It tells me whether it is windy,' responds Tim.

At that point I appear over Tim's other shoulder, with my hair being blown backwards fairly vigorously, and say, 'And is it?'

Tim looks at the device, with its pieces of paper and straw flying everywhere, and after a slight delay says, 'Yep.'

The third commercial I appeared in starts in the groundsman's shed. Don is wearing his jacket and is looking in the mirror straightening his tie as Tim walks in.

'Going on a hot date or something?' asks Tim.

'We have the sponsor's ambassador coming to see us, so you'd better tidy up this place and make it respectable,' Don replies.

'What would a banker know about cricket?' Tim says, playing some imaginary cricket shots with his bat.

'You'd be surprised,' says Don, as I appear at the door.

Don and I start to walk out of the shed, and as Tim follows, looking surprised and embarrassed, he hears me say to Don, 'Thanks for the piece of advice about coming off the short run in 1980.'

A chinaman

New Zealand was playing South Africa at Eden Park in the first test in 1999. South Africa amassed 621/5 declared, with Daryll Cullinan (275) beating Graeme Pollock's 274 to become the highest run-scorer in an innings in the history of South African cricket.

When New Zealand batted they replied with 352. Paul Adams, the unorthodox left-arm spinner whose technique has been described as like that of 'a frog in a blender', was bowling to Matt Horne. In the commentary box we were describing some of the types of deliveries Adams was bowling, including the googly or wrong 'un (where the ball spins the wrong way) and the chinaman. In cricket terminology a chinaman is a ball bowled by a left-arm bowler with the ball spinning from the off stump towards the leg stump with a wrist-spin action.

Television New Zealand received phone calls from several viewers who criticised the commentators for making racist comments, which surprised us a bit. Our director, Steve Coates, asked Glenn Turner to explain the meaning of the term 'chinaman' to viewers.

So Glenn explained, 'Paul Adams bowls a "chinaman", which is a ball bowled with a wrist-spin action by the left-arm spinner, with the ball pitching outside the line of the off stump and spinning in towards the right-handed batsman. It is cricket terminology that is quite common and no racist comments are intended. The term "chinaman" is named after a Chinese-West Indian cricketer, Achong, who played for the West Indies during the early 1930s. He bowled this type of unusual delivery, which was very different from those of other bowlers. The term "chinaman" became part of cricket language when an English batsman who had been dismissed was heard to say, "I have just been bowled by a chinaman." '

Commentators sometimes make reactionary comments, but fortunately no one came out with this one: 'Adams bowls a chinaman to Matt Horne, but there is no chink in his armour.'

A man of few words

John Arlott was recognised by many as the leading figure among England's radio and television commentators. He had magnificent timing, and his use of descriptive words was sparing but effective. One day he was describing Worcestershire's Ivan Johnson, a player from the Bahamas who was six foot tall (180 cm), as black as the ace of spades, and had a very distinctive Afro hairdo.

Worcester was playing a televised Sunday League match when the cameras panned in on Johnson. Arlott commented, 'There is the figure of Ivan Johnson fielding at fine leg. He is easily recognised by his sleeves, which are buttoned at the wrist.'

Rubbish or garbage!

The outstanding South African fielder Jonty Rhodes was fielding during a test at Eden Park when a plastic bag blew across the ground. Jonty picked up the bag, put it on his head, played with it, pretended to use it to catch the ball, then placed it in his pocket.

I was in the television commentary box with former New Zealand captain and opening batsman John Wright, watching Jonty play with the plastic bag. As the over neared its end Wrighty said, 'Jonty doesn't need a plastic bag to catch or stop the ball because his hands are exceptional. He stops and catches everything that comes his way.' Then, as the last ball of the over was bowled and we were about to go to a commercial break, with perfect timing Wrighty uttered one word: 'Garbage!'

The incident made me recall a story about Derek Randall, a magnificent fieldsman who played for Nottinghamshire and England. Derek was playing for Derek Robbin's XI against New Zealand in a festival match at Scarborough during the 1978 tour of England. Derek Randall, who is known as the 'clown prince' of world cricket, walked over to the boundary, picked up a wire-netting rubbish bin and placed it at cover. As the ball went up in the air, Randall stood in the rubbish bin and caught it.

Pay-back time

On the morning of the first day's play at Jade Stadium in Christchurch, after New Zealand had beaten South Africa at Carisbrook three days earlier, John Wright was interviewing the New Zealand coach, Steve Rixon.

'So, Steve, it'll be more of the same today then?' said Wrighty.

Steve Rixon looked somewhat surprised, and said, 'What sort of f… question was that?'

Wrighty was taken aback and everyone laughed, and the interview had to be started again.

Two weeks later Wrighty was doing his last interview before heading back to England to coach Kent. He decided to set up Steve Rixon, and get a pay-back in return for the previous interview.

The interview went well, and there was a slight pause before the final question.

'And Steve,' said Wrighty, 'is it true you taught Adam Parore to drive?'

'You bastard, Wrighty, you've got me there,' said Steve as he walked away chuckling, adding, 'I hope that's the end of the interview.'

Adam Parore had been caught allegedly driving at 170 kph in his BMW, and was to appear in court during the test.

Locked out!

Charlie Lock, a medium-pace bowler from Zimbabwe, had a day to remember at McLean Park, Napier, in 1995/96. He produced a fine spell of bowling, capturing the last four New Zealand wickets to end the day with 5/44 from 8.1 overs, thereby allowing Zimbabwe to win the day/night match by 21 runs.

New Zealand had looked set to win the match at 228 for five, but they lost their last four wickets for 18 runs when Charlie Lock dismissed Lee Germon for seven, Dipak Patel for four, Dion Nash for four, and Danny Morrison for one.

During a day/night at McLean Park between New Zealand and South Africa, I was in the radio commentary box with Neil Manthorp, a South African commentator. I was describing New Zealand's impressive record at the ground, where they had lost only two out of 13 matches, which also included a tied match. When I started to talk about the Zimbabwe match and the deeds of Charlie Lock, Neil couldn't believe his ears.

'Fancy Charlie Lock doing that,' he said. 'He's a nice fellow, but to get out to Charlie Lock is like being bitten by a sheep — it just shouldn't happen!'

Coneyisms!

Jeremy Coney, who captained New Zealand in the mid-1980s, was a very fine middle-order batsman. He is also a very talented after-dinner speaker. Once, describing his bowling during the 1983 World Cup in England, he said, 'My bowling is like autumn leaves — it just keeps fluttering down and the batsmen do not know whether to hit me for four or six, or to treat me with respect.'

In recent years Jeremy has become a successful radio commentator, whose wit and perceptive comments on the game are greatly enjoyed by many. During a test match at Wellington, New Zealand were in some difficulty as the South Africans were piling on the runs to reach 392/3. A deflated New Zealand team looked ragged in the field.

Jeremy was in the box as Chris Harris was delivering yet another ball in the series with very little success — at that point New Zealand had captured a total of nine wickets in the three-match series. Jeremy commented, 'There is Chris Harris, bowling another ball. It comes out of his hand like an inexperienced gynaecologist — a rather slow delivery.'

The village idiot!

Peter Walker played for Glamorgan and England before going on to become a noted television commentator. Like all commentators, he tried to do the right thing by being informative, constructive, opinionated and entertaining.

One day he received a letter from an annoyed viewer who disliked his commentaries, and who suggested that it might be a good idea if he retired. Peter ignored the letter and continued in his role, believing that he was still doing a good, honest job. A week later, the supervisor of the

BBC's cricket programmes received a letter from the same person, this time suggesting it would be a good idea if Mr Walker was removed from the commentary team. The letter went on to say, 'Mr Walker is a disgrace to the game. As well, he is robbing someone of being their village idiot.'

A bottle in the box

In addition to having a wonderful command of the English language, British commentator John Arlott was also very partial to a bottle of red wine or two. Before he went on air he would have some cheese and crackers and a bottle of the best wine he could find. By the end of the day he would have consumed three bottles.

He was once asked by his co-commentator, Peter Walker, 'John, how many bottles of red wine would you drink in a year?'

'About a thousand,' came the reply.

'That's nearly three bottles a day, John,' Peter said.

'Yes, that's right, Peter; but I also like a drop of white wine as well.'

Naivety is no excuse!

Charles Colville, a Sky TV sports commentator in the UK, was telling the story of some of his embarrassing moments in the commentary box, adding that every time commentators open their mouth in the 'box' there is trouble just around the corner.

The second women's one-day international between England and Australia was played at Grace Road, Leicester. In this age of political correctness commentators need to be careful to get things right so that no one is offended. Everything was going well this day until there was a fall of a wicket, when Charles said, 'She's got him!'

A short while later there was a huge cock-up (oops!) when a batting mix-up was described as, 'Total chaos here — both batsm… batsw… ah, persons are at the same end.'

When Somerset and England fast bowler Andy Caddick suffered from shin splints (sore shins that are very painful) during the 1994 tour of the West Indies, Charles had not heard of the term before. When he was interviewing Andy he naively asked, 'So how long have you been wearing them?'

Baby talk

During the 1999 World Cup in England the matches would start at 10.45 a.m., but for some matches the commentary on Radio Four long wave 198 did not start until 11.15 a.m. Britain's longest-running radio soap, *The Archers*, was on air during that half-hour period.

On this particular day the studio crossed over at 11.15 to the commentators at Headingley, where New Zealand were playing Zimbabwe in a 'Super Six' encounter. Christopher Martin Jenkins was describing to listeners what had happened in the first half-hour's play, to bring everyone up to date with the state of play. He then went on to talk about *The Archers*, giving Jeremy Coney, his co-commentator, an update on the programme and telling him how popular it was. Two of the most prominent characters had just had a baby, much to Jeremy's interest and delight, and he asked, 'How did they do that?'

Just as C.M.J. was about to expand on the situation Neil Johnson, the Zimbabwe opening batsman, was bowled by Geoff Allott.

C.M.J. said, 'He's out — he has been bowled.' A roar of laughter could be heard in the background of the commentary box, then there was a slight pause from C.M.J. before he went on to explain how Johnson had been dismissed.

Calling a spade a spade

At one time, Lance Cairns and I both wrote newspaper articles for different Sunday papers. Lance prefers to be more direct in his comments than me — I prefer to take what I see as a more positive and constructive point of view, whereas Lance tends to be more critical. I read his weekly columns with interest, and there are times when we agree with each other. There are also times when one or other of us will say something that stirs a reaction from readers, who make their feelings known in letters to the editor or when interviewed.

In an article published on 25 July 1999, I was amused by Lance's comments on some criticism he had received from Vaughan Johnson, a former first-class player who had become coach of the Wellington team. Lance took the opportunity to hit back in his column, writing:

Vaughan Johnson seems to be promoting himself as the new spokesman for the 'don't upset the apple-cart' brigade. This week he had some things to say about me, Warren Lees and Glenn Turner. He suggests we should pretend that Steve Rixon [the New Zealand coach] and Stephen Fleming [captain] don't make cock-ups. Craig McMillan, Fleming and Nathan Astle haven't been out of form [during the 1999 tour of England] and Rixon has the expertise to deal with out-of-form players.

He wants us to get in behind the team and support them. I am sure this guy [Johnson] is going to make a great coach. Imagine one of his batters getting his fifth duck in a row.

'Never mind,' he says. 'Today you have survived ten balls. It is just a matter of time and the runs will flow.'

Or the bowler who has just been belted for 50 runs in five overs. 'Don't worry,' says this great coach. 'Just think of the two balls they didn't score off.'

I don't like being told what to do by people who haven't got the guts to call a spade a spade.

The commentators are at it again!

The South African radio and television cricket commentators also have their share of mix-ups and malapropisms:

During a tense Benson and Hedges one-day match, Trevor Quirk commented, 'Alan Kourie, Transvaal's slow left-arm spin bowler, looks very calm at present, but inside his chest beats a heart.'

And during a test between the West Indies and South Africa at Bridgetown, Barbados: 'And there is the George Headley stand — it is named after George Headley.'

Louis Karpus during the World Cup: 'There are 25,000 people here today, and they are all here to watch the cricket.'

Nic Collis during a Currie Cup match: 'Omar Henry hit one or two boundaries in his seven.'

Martin Locke during the first test match of a series between India and South Africa: 'There is Anil Kumble. We are looking forward to seeing him bat, he is a very useful bowler.'

Michael Abrahamson during a match between India and a Combined XI: 'A very small crowd here today. I can count the people on one hand — can't be any more than thirty.'

Robin Jackman during a South African match against Sri Lanka at Colombo: 'Fourteen overs left — that's seven from each end.'

Martin Locke again: 'An emotional moment, a marvellous match, a terrific innings — what can one say on this historic day?'

And finally, Louis Karpus announcing a match at the WACA in Perth: 'We cross over now to the WACA for the match between Pakistan and Australia, where Richie Benaud is our commentator, so without further ado, it's over to the WACA, where Australia are playing Pakistan, our man, Richie Benaud, is waiting at the WACA, and it's Australia versus Pakistan, so over to you, Richie.'

Streaming the seam

The terminology used by cricket commentators is important when they are explaining the game to listeners or viewers. Some former players, however, have their own individual ways of getting the point across.

During the one-day tri-series in Singapore in 2000, Pakistan was playing South Africa in the final and Danny Morrison was describing the action as Jacques Kallis bowled to Ijaz Ahmed. 'He is streaming the seam,' he said, 'and he has fatted that one.'

For the purist: 'Jacques Kallis has bowled with the seam of the ball in a perpendicular or upright position and with it pitching on a good length in line with the off stump — and Ijaz Ahmed has hit the ball in the middle of the bat and it has gone for four runs.'

What a player!

Fred Trueman was the comments man on Radio Four as the New Zealand team were defeating England in an historic win at Lord's in July 1999.

Fred was talking about some of the great England batsmen of the past who would be turning in their graves at the current standard of England batting, which was mediocre to poor.

'Wally Hammond — what a great player he was. He was a great, great player. What a player. He was a great, great batsman — one of England's best. I never saw him play, but what a great player he was.'

Taking the knocks

I really enjoyed listening to Geoffrey Boycott's cricket commentaries during New Zealand's tour of India in 1999. For someone who as a player had a reputation for being dour, he actually has a good sense of humour. As a commentator he does, however, call the match as he sees it.

Sir Geoffrey got himself into trouble at a luxury French hotel in October 1996, later receiving a three-month suspended sentence for assault on his former girlfriend, Margaret Moore. She presented herself in public showing bruises on her face that she had apparently received from the assault, although to this very day Geoffrey swears black and blue that he didn't do it. Many of Geoffrey's supporters doubted whether he was capable of hitting her as many times as he did, because it would have taken him four hours to do it!

During the first test at Mohali, Indian fast bowler Javagal Srinath was giving New Zealand opening batsman Matt Horne a difficult time with some short-pitched deliveries. Boycs, in his Yorkshire accent, delivered his thoughts on the situation: 'It doesn't matter if he hits you in the ribs. It hurts, but not as much as getting out. Getting out hurts the rest of the day, the next day and the day after that. Bruises come and go, and they don't mean anything.'

Danny's at it again

Former New Zealand fast bowler Danny Morrison was also in India in 1999, commentating for Sky Television. Danny left many viewers bemused with his rather unusual choice of terminology:

'Sometimes it usually happens.'

'He was a tad unlucky that time.'

'He has made a pig of himself out there' (a comment directed at the free scoring of Indian Sachin Tendulkar, who was on his way to scoring a double century).

'He looks a bit stuffed out there in the middle at present' (the heat and humidity had taken their toll on Daniel Vettori as he completed his fifty-fourth over).

'That was a peach of a delivery' (well bowled).

Geoff Boycott, who was commentating with Danny, did say that this last description was new to him — the only food he had heard used to describe cricket was a 'jaffa', he said.

A sweet umpire!

During the second test between New Zealand and South Africa at Jade Stadium, Christchurch, in 1999, Martin Crowe was in the commentary box with the injured Chris Cairns, who was providing observations on the match.

New Zealand had been dismissed for a paltry 168 in the first innings and during a rain-affected match South Africa were 221/1, with Herchelle Gibbs and Jacques Kallis in control. The television cameras panned in on umpire David Quested, who was sucking a sweet. Roger Twose was standing nearby as Crowe went on to say, 'There is David Quested, standing in his third test match. It is great to see him take the time to talk to players between balls, which helps him, and the players around him, to stay relaxed.'

Chris Cairns, who knew exactly what was going on, said to Martin, 'All Twosey wants is a lolly!'

Hooked out

Former Australian left-handed batsman David Hookes was a guest commentator for Sky Television during the Australian cricket team's tour of New Zealand in 2000. After being in the country for five weeks, Hooksey was on air on the last day of the tour, as the Australians were defeating the Black Caps 3–0 in the test series. The Australians had also won the one-day series 4–1, so they had completely outplayed, out-thought and outskilled the New Zealanders. The Australian supporters were obviously very impressed with their team's performances.

Not so the New Zealand supporters. Hooksey read out a letter he had received: 'This letter is addressed to me from Sandra Gibson in Ashburton. She has to be a Miss Gibson, because you would not want to be married to her. It says, "Dear Mr Hookes, you and [radio commentator] Jim Maxwell are the pits! Why don't you both go back to Australia and leave the commentary to the New Zealanders?"'

Hooksey's response to the letter was short and to the point: 'The answer is quite simple, Miss Gibson. You could change the channel and watch the cartoons.'

extras

Cricket lovers

Cricketers are reputed to be good lovers. They are fast between the covers and they don't go in without protection.

A selectorial problem

An out-of-form New Zealand cricketer was asked who his greatest opponent was.

'The New Zealand team selectors,' was his reply.

Your steak, sir!

An unnamed cricketer received a black eye from a short rising ball. Later he was introduced to Her Majesty the Queen, who told him, 'I think you should put some steak on that eye to reduce the swelling.'

'In our country, ma'am, we eat our steaks,' came the reply.

Well beaten

A young boy whose parents were getting divorced was asked by the judge, 'Would you like to live with your father?'

'No,' the boy said. 'My father beats me.'

'Would you like to live with your mother?' asked the judge.

'No, Your Honour, she beats me too.'

'Well!' said the judge. 'Who would you like to live with?'

'The English cricket team — they can't beat anyone,' said the boy.

An appointment

A cricketer went to the doctor and said, 'I have a problem, doctor. I can't bat, I can't bowl and I can't field. What do you think I should do?'

The doctor suggested, 'I think you should take some time off from the game, have a rest and do something else.'

'I can't do that,' said the cricketer. 'I'm playing for England in the second test at the MCG tomorrow.'

Fixed match

After the match-fixing allegations involving disgraced South African captain Hansie Cronje, the gags inevitably started to flow.

'You walk into a dark room and the electricity is out. All you've got is one candle and one match. In your haste to light the candle, the match breaks. What do you do?'

Answer: 'Call Hansie … he'll fix it.'

The chairman knows where to go

I was appointed chairman of the New Zealand Cricket selection panel in July 2000. During the next nine months the team and some individuals in particular experienced rather mixed results. The media criticised many of our selections and our long-term vision of developing the players and the game to make the team more competitive. Quite a few members of the public expressed their views about the job I was doing — some wrote complimentary letters; others, such as the following letter, were not.

Richard Hadlee

C/- NZ Cricket

Christchurch

The bloody quicker that you get your nose out of the running of the cricket, then all the better NZ will be for it. You poke your bloody nose in where it is definitely not wanted. We have the players out there to make a 1st class NZ team. Both in test cricket and also in the one-dayers if you kept your bloody nose out of it and let the selectors pick a team. You are just a one-sided so and so and talk a lot of shit when you are interviewed but everyone in NZ can understand that though, as everyone knows just how one-eyed you can be. You couldn't pick your nose let alone pick a cricket team. We have got the players here so let the ones who know something about cricket get on with it. You are just a bowler and not a cricketer.

None of us will go to a cricket match now seeing that you are trying to run it by poking your nose in all of the time. Look how the attendances have dropped all threw [*sic*] you. Get real man and get out from where you are not needed. Our club runs 100% because it is run properly and not like yours. Just because your name is Hadlee don't get a swollen head. Get down to earth man.

R.K.

Running the game

There is always a lot of pressure on umpires to get decisions right and to be consistent with their decision-making. Where possible, it is best to have a neutral person doing the umpiring, to avoid any suggestion of bias, but in some matches players have to do their own umpiring. Understandably, their integrity is often questioned, especially in a close game when the batting team's umpire gives one of his own players 'not out' to a very confident lbw decision.

During one match an elderly gentleman offered his assistance, saying, 'I have never umpired a match before. Do I have to run with the ball?'

One of the players responded, 'No, only after the match if you get some of the decisions wrong.'

A woman's point of view

England's Rachel Hayhoe-Flint, a top-order batswoman and an England captain, is regarded as the world's finest women's cricketer. She was once asked what she thought of coaches.

'Professional coaching is a man trying to get you to keep your legs together, when other men spend a lifetime trying to keep them apart.'

Barmy Army!

England's Barmy Army travel the world to support the England cricket team, no doubt annoying many locals with their chant, 'Barmy Army, Barmy Army, Barmy Army.' Opposition players often cop quite a bit of flak, especially the Australians, with comments such as 'If grandad was deported, clap your hands' directed at their convict roots.

Australia's Mark Waugh and Shane Warne came under fire after they admitted they had been fined by the Australian Cricket Board for accepting money from a bookie during the tour of India and Pakistan in 1994. The ACB had kept the scandal quiet, but the Barmy Army seized the opportunity to stir matters up, singing a song to the tune of 'My Old Man's a Dustman'. The chant goes:

> Mark Waugh is an Aussie,
> He wears a baggy cap.
> And when he saw the bookies' cash,
> He said, 'I am having some of that.'
>
> He shared it out with Warney.
> They went and had some beers.
> And when the ACB found out,
> They covered it up for years.

Permit me to make a point

A self-styled 'cricket fanatic' wrote a letter similar to the one I received, disagreeing with the selectors' faith in captain Stephen Fleming.

> The Selectors
> New Zealand Cricket
> Dear Sirs
> I am a cricket fanatic and an oldie so trust you will permit me to make the following comments.
> One reason why Australia is so good at sports is that their selectors are hardheaded to the extent that the country comes ahead of individuals. Hence the sacking of the Waugh brothers.

I wish to put forward several reasons why Stephen Fleming should be dropped right away from our one day cricket team.

1. He is not a good captain. His mind is too slow and rigid. We can have an opponent on the ropes ready for the kill and he lets them back into the game.

2. He is too tough on his bowlers with the result we have more injuries than any other country.

3. That he is dull is borne out by his remarks a few weeks ago. Referring to his batting he said 'I am in good touch and have an average of 48.' It was not mentioned that every time he scored over 40 the team lost. Because of his slow rate of scoring, too big a task was left his team mates to score a win. Take the 4th game against the English. We had to score 245 off 300 balls, a rate of 82. He faced about 117 balls at a rate of 67. Did he expect the rest of the team including the bowlers to average a rate of 92 to make up for his pedestrian scoring? Many of them went out for a low score trying to make up for him. Looking at the score sheet did not he do well??

4. Let us look at the 5th game. Fleming faced 12 balls. 11 dots and one run. Our scoring rate was 6 per over when he went in. When he came out it had dropped in that short time to 5. Thank goodness he went out. When he went in the batsmen were on top. When he went out the bowlers were on top. As in other games when he went out cheaply we usually won. And we won the game he did not play in.

5. If you want to do well in the world cup and of course you do, be like the Aussies and act now. Drop him from the one day squad without delay.

We need partnerships, but I would hate to be his partner. The game goes off the boil and the opposing bowlers love it, which makes it doubly hard for his partner.

Yours sincerely

Takin' a dim view of things

Spectators pay a lot of money to be entertained by professional cricketers, and they have the right to express their views, whether favourable or not. Some spectators also entertain themselves, their companions and the players with some very clever calls.

'Rowdy' Ashley Mallett, Australia's off-spin bowler during the 1970s, never had too much to say, but his team-mates enjoyed the numerous opportunities for humour that arose as a result of his mishaps and his personality. It seemed he was a walking disaster, and many people took advantage of situations in which he was involved.

Rowdy sometimes wore contact lenses when he played cricket, but on other occasions he wore his prescription tinted glasses. During a tour of the West Indies he wore his glasses, and after he had bowled a few deliveries in the test a local yelled out, 'Hey, Mr Mallett mon. You takin' a dim view of this match.'

We will win one soon

A village cricket team was struggling to compete and were desperate to start winning some games. After advertising for a professional to join the team they were delighted to sign a Chinese player, who was called Win One Soon.

Win made a dramatic impact by capturing 6/12 in his first match after scoring 69 with the bat. A little later his brother sent him a telegram asking if he had won any matches. Win replied, 'We won one and we will some more.'

Can you name this Pakistan team?

I work as a public relations ambassador for the Bank of New Zealand, which sponsored and supported New Zealand cricket through the 1990s. During lunch intervals at the cricket we would sometimes have trivia competitions in the corporate hospitality area, and I would have to come up with original questions. This was not always easy, since the same guests often returned to share the BNZ's hospitality.

One year I asked, 'Can you name the 1979 Pakistan cricket team?'

The guests were obviously having a little difficulty answering the question, so to have a little fun I started to name a possible team: 'Majid Khan, Mohsin Khan, Imran Khan, Rashid Khan, Azhar Khan, Javed Miandad Khan, Liaqat Ali Khan, Zakir Khan … Genghis Khan, the Aga Khan …'

They soon get the hang of it after that, and came up with an inspired list of team members.

An ambitious request from a fan

21/11/89

Dear Richard

I have a lot of free time at the moment, so I thought that I would drop you a note.

I have been a fan of yours for many years — in fact, I really enjoyed watching you beat the Australians at Eden Park in 1987.

I love the game very much. As a youngster I played the game and I was the best player in my team, which was the 4th XI.

When I left school, my game improved and I captained my club team to win the Third Grade B competition.

I always had ambitions of playing test cricket for New Zealand, but somehow I think it is too late for me now — I am 63.

I listen to all the games on radio and sometimes I watch the TV. It is difficult to get down to the grounds these days, because they prefer to keep me in at weekends.

I live in Auckland, in fact I am based at Mount Eden (Prison).

I still have three more years to serve on an aggravated burglary charge.

I would dearly love to have a memento of yours, perhaps a signed playing shirt so that I can remember your achievements.

Yours sincerely

A cricket fan

P.S. If it helps, the house I burgled was owned by an Australian.

The intense disciple: Richard Hadlee shade of light

The following poem by Robin McConnell appears in *nothing is as physical as a poem*, published by The Pohutukawa Press in 1997.

In the frame
A familiar side step

Initials a signature

Marking summer toil

Measured by a lean limbed metronome

Beating time and the opening bat

In a parabola of swing

Uncoiling

From the body hard whip

Wielded by this intense disciple

Of efficiency

With every excess motion purged by a five day sun

To reveal a paradox in white

A miser

Dispensing gold coinage of the realm

Or minimal artist

Who engraves a singular line

And yet fills the eye's rich canvas

With all of Richard Hadlee

Shade of light.

Antarctic cricketers

At a luncheon in Christchurch the guest speaker was talking about some of the great Antarctic expeditions, including those of the Norwegian Amundsen and the Englishman Robert Falcon Scott.

The vote of thanks was given by a member of the Christchurch Businessmen's Club, who finished by asking, 'What do Antarctic explorers and Australian cricketers have in common?'

Answer: 'They are both good at sledging.'

On hallowed ground

Some time ago I received the following letter from the organisers of an event called 'On Hallowed Ground — The Great Canterbury Dinner'. Honoured as I was, I did wonder whether they had sent it to the right person.

Dear Sir Richard

We're pleased to announce that you have been nominated for an exciting new award that seeks to recognise individuals who have made a difference to life in Canterbury. Named 'Canterbury's First Fifteen', it will be launched at a gala charity event at Jade Stadium on May 4th 2002.

Appropriately, the award has fifteen categories:

Architecture

Commerce

Education

Entrepreneur

Environmentalist

Fashion

Law

Literature

Media

Performing arts

Politics

Technology

Sport (female)

Sport (male)

Visual arts

You have been nominated in the category of Sport (female).

To assist in the judging process, we invite you to submit a short biography and a photograph of yourself.

[…]

Yours sincerely

Coming to terms with sailing

Having been involved with cricket all my life, there were times when I needed to step outside my comfort zone and learn about other sports. I love rugby, league, golf, tennis and soccer and I consider myself reasonably well informed about those games, but when it comes to America's Cup yachting it is another story.

I had the great pleasure of being involved with Team New Zealand's defence of the 'Auld Mug' in 2000. The Bank of New Zealand, like many companies, wanted to be part of the event and the occasion. We decided to hire a 120-passenger ferry boat and entertain some clients on board while the races were in progress. We also contracted some yachting personalities to give us some expert commentary on board and to entertain our guests. Chris Dickson, Bret de Thier and Joe Butterfield did an outstanding job in explaining the history of the cup, yachting terminology, tactics and their thoughts on who would win — Prada or Team New Zealand.

As the Bank of New Zealand ambassador it was my job to introduce the commentary team and to host our guests on each of the five days we were out on the water. I felt like the 'Admiral' of the Royal Bank of New Zealand Yacht Squadron Team, until Chris Dickson said, 'Yes, Admiral Richard, I looked the word "Admiral" up in the dictionary, and I noted that it is red and white, meaning "butterfly" '. My ego suffered a temporary set-back, but I was able to recover and survive.

I felt it was important to do some homework and familiarise myself with some yachting terminology so that I didn't embarrass myself too much. With the help of our 'experts', I learnt the following common sailing terms:

Bow: A form of introduction employed by Japanese sailors. Also refers to the front or pointy end of the boat.

Capsize: A unit of hat measurement. Also the act of a yacht rolling onto its side and depositing all the crew into the water.

Close-hauled: A Scottish expression. Everything on the vessel is 'tight' — the sheets, the sails, the owner and the helmsman. Also refers to a vessel sailing as close to the wind as possible.

Genoa: An Australian term from a Sydney-based sailor, based on the expression used on learning that a certain young lady is not necessarily his alone — 'Do yuh know a?' Also refers to a large sail at the front of the boat.

Gybe: Verbal banter. Also a term used to describe a boat's move away from the wind sufficient that the wind catches the reverse side of the mainsail.

Keel: After having a few drinks on board, some sailors 'keel over'. Also, a large bulbous item found on the bottom of boats to keep them upright.

Ketch: Australian cricketers are heard to say 'ketch' when a ball is hit into the air. Also, a two-masted yacht.

Lee-o: A star sign. Also a warning to fellow sailors that you are about to 'go about'.

Mark: A high-pitched shriek uttered by rugby players upon catching the ball in their own 25-m zone. Also the floaty thing a boat sails around.

Bottom mark: An unpleasant consequence of a frightening mishap if a sailor fails to reach the loo in time. Some cricketers experience this embarrassing situation in places like India and Pakistan. Also refers to the end mark of the course.

Top mark: What nasty swots get at school. Also the mark at the other end of the course, opposite to the bottom mark.

Mizzen: Absent without leave. Also the mast behind the main mast on vessels with more than one mast.

Overboard: Refers to sailors' wives who go over the top when their husbands come home late or have had too much to drink. Also a term meaning that a crew member has temporarily or permanently placed himself or herself outside the confinements of the boat and is spending time in the water.

Point: An Australian term for a unit of beer. Also to sail close to the wind.

Reach: To stretch out one's arm for offered refreshments. Also refers to those points of sailing between 'close-hauled' and 'running'.

Round: An unspecified number of drinks. Also the act of negotiating a marker buoy.

Running: A frantic attempt to reach the boat before it leaves the dock. Also sailing with the wind behind the boat.

Schooner: An Australian term for a large glass of beer. Also a type of yacht with one or two masts.

Sheet: An Australian term for being in trouble; e.g. 'Jeez, mate, you're in the sheet now.' Being 'between the sheets' is a favourite pastime of most mariners. Being caught between the sheets with a crew member of the opposite sex is also an activity that leads to 'man overboard'. Sheet is also another silly term given to a bit of rope attached to the clew of a sail.

Sloop: The sound emitted when attempting to drink hot soup in rough weather. Also refers to a yacht that has one mast.

Spinnaker: Unsatisfactory outcome of cornering with a motor vehicle at high speed. Also a large sail used for sailing downwind.

Starboard: Why Rachel left Rod Stewart. Also refers to the right-hand side of the boat. A starboard marker is painted green and should be to the right of a vessel when it enters the harbour.

Stay: The order given to the batsman at the non-striker's end to stay in his crease when there is no chance of a run. Also a thin metal rope which, together with its partners, is designed to stop the mast falling down.

Stern: The look on a partner's face following a mariner's late return. Also the back end of a boat.

Tack: Content of a tasteless joke. Also a form of sailing in a zig-zag fashion in an attempt to sail into the wind.

Tell-tale: Evidence such as lipstick on a collar or a stain on a dress that annoys the person who has been dishonest. Also a device to indicate which way the wind is blowing.

Tiller: What a sailor with a girl in every port fails to tell his wife. Also a stick thing that steers small yachts.

Wave: A mariner's signal involving the hand and the arm, used to say goodbye to the family prior to leaving the dock. Also refers to the momentum of the sea that results in a sudden surge on the top of the water, causing it to break.

Winch: A derogatory expression applied to a female crew member. Also a device for pulling or tightening ropes.

The Sir Richard Hadlee Collection

Visit our website at www.hadlee.co.nz for more information about Sir Richard, Hadlee cricket equipment and Hadlee memorabilia.

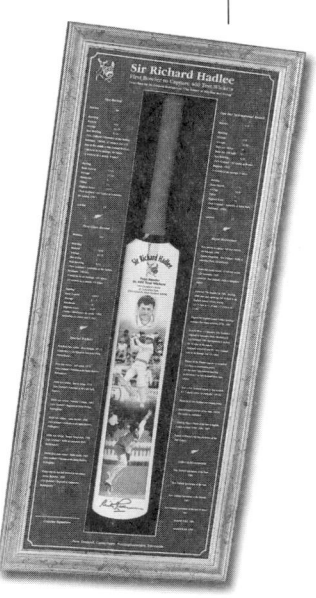